enlighten

WELCOME TO ENLIGHTEN

Here at Enlighten our mission is simple. We assist others in transformative healing by sharing the amazing benefits of essential oils. As certified facilitators and students of a variety of energy modalities, our founders offer unique perspectives on combining clinical techniques with powerful all-natural tools. This bestselling book was the very first published on the subject and has been well loved and referenced often.

VISIT OUR WEBSITE

We'll help you discover the depth of essential oils in new and profound ways.

Stop by *www.enlightenhealing.com,* where you'll find additional tools and resources for training, events, and webinars.

Sharing Is Caring — Bulk Discounts Available
Interested in sharing *Emotions & Essential Oils* with your clients, family members, and teams? We offer bulk order discounts starting at just 25 copies! Contact us at **customerservice@enlightenhealing.com** for more information.

Emotions & Essential Oils
A REFERENCE GUIDE FOR EMOTIONAL HEALING
Sixth Edition

ISBN 978-0-9991549-1-5

Printed in the USA

PUBLISHED BY:

Enlighten Alternative Healing, LLC
P.O. Box 520191, Salt Lake City, Utah 84152-0191
www.enlightenhealing.com

NOTICE TO READERS

"The medical school of the future will not particularly interest itself in the ultimate results and products of disease, nor will it pay so much attention to actual physical lesions, or administer drugs and chemicals merely for the sake of palliating our symptoms, but knowing the true cause of sickness and aware that the obvious physical results are merely secondary, it will concentrate its efforts upon bringing about that harmony between body, mind and soul which results in the relief and cure of disease."

"Amongst the types of remedies that will be used will be those obtained from the most beautiful plants and herbs to be found in the pharmacy of Nature, such as have been divinely enriched with healing powers for the mind and body of man."

— Dr. Edward Bach, *Heal Thyself: An Explanation of the Real Cause and Cure of Disease* (1931)

EMOTIONS &
ESSENTIAL OILS

A REFERENCE GUIDE FOR
EMOTIONAL HEALING

WHERE DO ESSENTIAL OILS COME FROM?

Essential oils are highly concentrated versions of the powerful natural oils found in various parts of plants. Refer to these symbols for information on the specific origin of the single oils included in this book.

 BARKS & WOODS

 PEELS

 FRUITS & BERRIES

 RESINS

 FLOWERS

 ROOTS

 LEAVES & NEEDLES

 SEEDS

Plants featured in *Emotions & Essential Oils* botanical illustrations:
Title Page — jasmine, lavender, and ylang ylang
Section I — basil, rosemary, and eucalyptus
Section II — juniper berry
Section III — bergamot, grapefruit, and lemon
Section IV — birch, cedarwood, and sandalwood

TABLE OF CONTENTS

SECTION I: HEALING WITH ESSENTIAL OILS

SECTION II: SINGLE OILS

Introduction

SECTION III: OIL BLENDS

Introduction

SECTION IV: APPENDICES

SECTION I

HEALING WITH ESSENTIAL OILS

KALLIE'S STORY

The following true story, written by Kallie's mother, perfectly embodies the steps involved in emotional healing—from the time of trauma through the healing crisis and on to wholeness. It beautifully illustrates how the use of essential oils facilitates physical, emotional, and spiritual healing. We sincerely thank Kallie and her family for allowing their story to be included in this book.

When my daughter Kallie was two years old, she accidentally pulled a slow cooker full of boiling meat down onto herself, severely burning her face and torso. Second- and third-degree burns covered a third of her body. For a month, Kallie recuperated in a special burn unit where she received heavy narcotics along with other medications to help numb the intense pain that accompanies such severe burns. Two surgeries were necessary to place skin grafts on her face, neck, and shoulders. When Kallie finally came home, she had to wear a plastic mask on her face and a tight-fitting body suit for six months to keep the skin grafts from warping.

As her mother, it was horrifying to see my child suffer so much pain; I felt helpless. But Kallie was a very strong girl who tried her best to adapt to the excruciating medical procedures, such as having the dead skin scrubbed from the burned area or working through physical therapy. During the many times when the pain and trauma were too much for little Kallie, she would mentally leave us. I could see it in her hollow eyes. The first time I saw this was when the initial burn happened. In those few seconds right after the hot liquid touched her precious skin, she wasn't there. Due to the combination of heavy narcotics and unbearable procedures, she was physically and emotionally numb or just plain absent during most of the month that she was hospitalized. After we got home, it took a while to get back to regular life. Kallie was just so fragile and delicate. I tried my absolute best to physically and emotionally help her and our family recover from this event, but it was quite a challenge.

The months and years went by, and I started to notice that Kallie was extremely numb to pain. She was a very active, adventurous girl and had quite a few falls and injuries just like any other child, but she rarely acknowledged that it hurt her. Sometimes it was disturbing. I remember one visit to the doctor for her regular vaccines. Kallie lay down on the table, and the two nurses poked both her legs two times each. I watched her face and there was absolutely no physical or emotional reaction whatsoever. She was unfeeling. She often got nasty gashes or scrapes, and I wouldn't even know about them until later when I gave her a bath or changed her clothes. I would ask her where she got hurt and a lot of times she didn't even remember. She was also very self-conscious of the physical changes the burn had caused. When Kallie began school, she tried to hide her scars by covering them with her hair or coat or by walking with her face pointed toward the wall and away from onlookers.

I never pushed her to talk about it or do anything that was uncomfortable for her, but I gently tried to give her opportunities to share her thoughts and feelings. When Kallie was about five and a half, she started to forget what happened. She knew that something big occurred a long time ago, but she couldn't remember the details. Sometimes there was a trigger that sparked her memory, like the word "burn," or a fire, or even a bath. Then with fear and confusion in her eyes she would start asking, "What happened to me, Mom?" Around this time, I was introduced to essential oils. As my mother and I learned about the oils and their benefits, we thought of Kallie. Helichrysum and Vetiver seemed like the perfect fit, and we began treatment. I was so excited in the beginning, mostly thinking of the potential physical healing and largely unaware of the emotional benefits. Kallie was full of faith. She immediately said, "I know it's going to make my burn melt away, Mom!" I had no idea what was coming.

After only a few days of using the oils, Kallie started to act differently. The first thing I noticed was that she started to complain of physical pain for which we could find no reasonable explanation. Every time she would get the smallest cut or bruise, she had major anxiety about it—very opposite from her recent tough, numb-to-pain reactions. She cried for hours about tiny cuts or slivers and would say through tears, "Is it ever going to go away?" Kallie spent a large portion of the day worrying about the smallest things. It was almost impossible to convince her to take a bath. She became extremely picky about the clothes she wore. If clothing touched her "wrong" or was at all tight, she wouldn't wear it. Any mention of her being burned or even the word "burn" caused extreme fear. Anxiety attacks surfaced. Sometimes she randomly sat on my lap and just cried. I would cry too.

I finally realized Kallie was going through a healing crisis brought on by the oils. It made perfect sense. Every odd thing that she was doing directly correlated to the burn or to her experience in the hospital. With the help of essential oils, her body was expelling or ejecting all of the pain and hidden emotions that were buried for so long.

We guessed that the healing would probably last for the same amount of time she had stayed in the hospital. This was exactly right. It lasted a month. I tried my best to validate what she was feeling and to help her as much as I could during this time. I learned that if I missed a day of putting on her oils, it was a bad day for her and the rest of the household! So, I kept up with it and the results were phenomenal.

After this difficult month, I began to notice that words which had previously triggered a negative reaction from Kallie did not seem to bother her. She had a totally new and positive perspective. I could see plain as day that she was no longer coming from a place of fear. Instead of being self-conscious or shy, she was secure, strong, and confident—a totally different Kallie.

As her mom, I can see without a doubt that these essential oils gave her such a beautiful new outlook on herself and her past traumatic experience. On the morning of Kallie's seventh birthday, I was telling her about the day she was born, and she said, "I don't remember that, Mom, but I do remember when I was burned." I carefully asked, "What do you feel when you remember it?" She replied in her bubbly, secure voice, "Let me spell it for you mom: OK!" Words cannot express how very grateful I am that my little Kallie could heal emotionally.

FIVE STAGES OF HEALING

As illustrated in Kallie's story, essential oils play a powerful role in emotional healing. They lead us by the hand as we courageously face our emotional issues. Kallie is not the only one with repressed emotional trauma. We all hold unresolved feelings of pain and hurt which need to be brought to the surface for transformation and healing.

Essential oils support healing in five stages. They strengthen us during each stage and prepare us for the next level of healing. For example, as we regain our physical health, we are invited to enter the emotional realm. In this manual, we briefly explore stages one, three, four, and five; however, the main focus of this book is stage two: the emotional stage.

FIVE STAGES OF HEALING:

1. Essential oils assist in healing the physical body.

2. Essential oils assist in healing the heart.

3. Essential oils assist in releasing limiting beliefs.

4. Essential oils increase spiritual awareness and connection.

5. Essential oils inspire the fulfillment of our life's purpose.

STAGE ONE: HEALING THE PHYSICAL BODY
Essential oils are powerful physical healers. Some essential oils are considered to be 40–60 times more potent than herbs.[1] Essential oils assist the body in fighting unfriendly microorganisms; purifying organs, glands, and body systems; balancing body functions; and raising the body's energetic vibration.[2]

STAGE TWO: HEALING THE HEART
As the oils secure our physical health, they provide us with the energy needed to penetrate the heart and enter the emotional realm. Essential oils raise the vibration of the physical body.[3] As the body lives in higher energetic vibrations, lower energies (such as suppressed

emotions) become unbearable. The body wants to release these feelings. Stagnant anger, sadness, grief, judgment, and low self-worth cannot exist in the environment of balance and peace which essential oils help to create.

Emotional healing occurs as old feelings surface and release.[4] Sometimes this experience is confused with regression. People may perceive they are going backward or that the essential oils are not working. We are so used to symptomatic healing that we have been conditioned to view healing as the immediate cessation of all physical and emotional pain. In reality, the oils are working. They are working to permanently heal emotional issues by supporting individuals through their healing.

Principles of Healing: Release and Receive
It is important to understand that healing is a process. The process can be separated into two main principles: release and receive.

We must release trapped negative emotions before we can receive positive feelings. The old must go to make space for the new. We often want to skip this step, but it is a necessary one. We must be willing to experience the cleansing if we truly desire healing. Resisting the cleansing process makes healing more painful. We must surrender to the experience so that we may continue on the path of healing. The more we let go and trust, the more enjoyable this healing process can be.

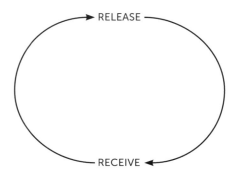

Essential Oils Don't Do Our Emotional Work for Us

Essential oils assist individuals in taking an honest look within. They foster the right environment for healing, but they will not do the work for us. In gardening, it is a common mistake to pull the weeds while leaving the roots. This is particularly true for hard and rocky soils. To ensure we uproot the whole plant, we can add water to the soil, which allows the entire weed to be removed. Similarly, essential oils prepare our emotional soil so that weeds may be removed with greater ease. However, they do not do the weeding for us. If we neglect to do the work of pulling our weeds, we have simply watered the problem. On the other hand, when we combine essential oils with emotional work, we reap the fruits of our labor.

STAGE THREE: RELEASING LIMITING BELIEFS

Unlike emotions, which are temporary in nature, beliefs are long term and deeply rooted in our subconscious. Beliefs are our deeply held framework that is forged from the conclusions we make about our experiences. This belief framework forms the lens through which we see life. For better or worse, our beliefs about ourselves are what we use to define our identity. This has far-reaching effects on all our behavior, thoughts, and emotional patterns. All of us have positive and negative beliefs. However, our negative or limiting beliefs can cause the same issues to reoccur over and over throughout our lives. Repeated experiences reinforce the associated emotional pathways. Essential oils assist in illuminating the emotional patterns of deeply held beliefs, encouraging us to identify what the limiting beliefs are, releasing the trapped energy and associated emotions, and, finally, replacing them with positive beliefs that will serve our highest good.

STAGE FOUR: SPIRITUAL AWARENESS & CONNECTION

All beings were created with divine intention. Acknowledgment of our spiritual nature and connection to our source is an essential part of healing. Most important in this stage is the awareness of the specific intention for us and infinite love available to us. It is from this love that our healing can become complete.

STAGE FIVE: LIFE'S PURPOSE

When we have experienced the previous four aspects—necessary in truly holistic healing—we are now ready to fully actualize our purpose and potential. This stage is where we achieve the clarity and courage to follow the path that is meant for us.

1. Schnaubelt, K. (2011). *The Healing Intelligence of Essential Oils.* (pp. 13-16). Rochester, VT: Healing Arts Press.

2. Stewart, D. (2003). *Healing Oils of the Bible.* (pp. 31-34). Marble Hill, MO: Care Publications.

3. Stewart, D. (pp. 31-34).

4. Moreton, V. S. (1992). *A New Day in Healing!* (pp. 16-17). San Diego, CA: Kalos Publishing.

A WORD ON QUALITY

THREE CATEGORIES OF ESSENTIAL OILS:
1. Aromatic Essential Oils
2. Therapeutic-Grade Essential Oils
3. Independently Tested Therapeutic-Grade Essential Oils

The first category applies to many oils marketed for their scent and aromatic properties. These essential oils are widely available in health food stores. It is important to know that these essential oils are often not therapeutic grade and should not be used topically or internally, as they are not for medicinal use. These oils are usually synthetic and therefore harmful to the body. They have no therapeutic value.

The second category of essential oils is therapeutic-grade oils. Many companies fall into this category. The intent of these companies is to provide quality essential oils that can be used for healing. These oils are for topical and aromatic use. Great care should be taken when purchasing these oils, as they are often diluted with synthetic chemicals or other additives.

The third category of essential oils is independently tested therapeutic-grade oils for aromatic or topical use. These oils are tested at independent laboratories with tests such as gas chromatography and mass spectrometry to verify their purity and composition. Oils that meet rigorous testing and are considered safe by the Food and Drug Administration may also be considered for internal use. Never use any essential oil internally that is not Generally Recognized as Safe (GRAS) for dietary consumption by the FDA. Consult with a healthcare practitioner. Only the highest-quality and purest essential oils should be used for physical, emotional, and spiritual healing.

TOOLS FOR EMOTIONAL WORK

There are several great aids to assist you when beginning your emotional work. We suggest these tools in addition to essential oils to facilitate the healing process.

MEDITATION

Regardless of method, most mindfulness-based practices have a positive effect on mental and emotional well-being. Choose any method that resonates with you and practice it consistently to enhance the benefits of all other emotional healing practices. Meditation practitioners find that the benefits are compounded over time.

JOURNALING

Keeping any kind of journal can be beneficial. Three main journaling techniques include keeping a gratitude journal; free writing (or stream-of-consciousness journaling); or letter writing, where you work out your feelings in a letter to someone (not necessarily to be mailed). Writing your thoughts and feelings eases mental strain, releases stagnant energy, lifts dark moods, inspires creative and diverse thought, increases self-esteem, and invites calm. It's a powerful tool for processing all types of emotional content.

PERSONAL INVENTORY

This time-honored technique involves making a self-assessment: listing personal strengths and positive qualities on one side of a chart and weaknesses or blocks to success on the other. This will help you acknowledge what's working in your life (often the most important part of the process) and help you to identify what's out of balance. A deep and honest moral inventory is part of most 12-step recovery programs.

NATURE THERAPY

Recent science is reporting that significant benefits come from spending time outdoors in any context from exercising to relaxing to meditating. Walking barefoot in grass or sand, putting your hands in soil, strolling in natural areas with lots of trees—even watching beautiful nature films or art portraying nature—can make you feel grounded, centered, and more at peace.

PERSONALIZED MODALITIES

From music therapy, play therapy, and talk therapy to energy work, regression work, and subconscious work, there are a variety of modalities and therapies that can assist emotional healing and recovery. Feel free to pair essential oils with any practice that personally works for you.

Additionally, all emotional work is enhanced by building on a strong base of physical health. You don't need to wait until you have faultless physical health habits in order to begin. Try to give yourself the nutrition, exercise, and especially the sleep that you need, and you will see even greater benefits from your essential oils.

HOW TO USE ESSENTIAL OILS

Please reference all safety information from the manufacturer or a competent reference book when using essential oils for aromatic, topical, or internal use.

AROMATIC

To use an essential oil aromatically, simply smell the oil directly from the bottle. Or place a few drops into a diffuser, which disperses the oil into the air. Another option is to add a few drops into the palms of the hands, rub together, and inhale.

TOPICAL

To use an essential oil topically, add a few drops in the palm of the hand with a carrier oil and apply to the selected area. Essential oils are very potent, so a small amount should be sufficient. Due to their volatility (rapid evaporation), diluting essential oils with a carrier oil is recommended; dilution is especially recommended for those with sensitive skin, including children and babies. Dilution does not reduce the effects of essential oils; rather it increases their effectiveness. Some oils may not be safe for children or during pregnancy or while nursing. If you are pregnant or nursing, consult a healthcare practitioner before using essential oils.

INTERNAL

Oils that are Generally Recognized as Safe (GRAS) by the Food and Drug Administration may be considered for dietary consumption. Never take any essential oil internally that is not considered safe by the FDA. Consult a healthcare practitioner before internal use.

HOW TO USE THIS BOOK

OIL DESCRIPTIONS
The main body of this manual is divided into individual descriptions of the oils. Single oils are listed first followed by blends. Read the descriptions to determine which essential oil would be best suited for your emotional needs.

DECODING EMOTIONS
If you're unsure how to identify which emotion you are feeling, start in Decoding Emotions (Appendix A) to match up your physical and emotional symptoms.

NEGATIVE EMOTIONS AND POSITIVE PROPERTIES
You can use the Negative Emotions and Positive Properties chart (Appendix B) in three ways to quickly scan the emotions and properties related to each oil. First, you can search through the listed oils. Second, you can search the negative properties for what you're struggling with now. Third, you can search the positive properties for what you would like to invite into your life. Each oil has at least three positives and three negatives listed.

EMOTIONS INDEX
Additionally, you can search the comprehensive Emotions Index (Appendix C) to find specific emotional states and the recommended oils which support those states.

EMOTIONS AND ESSENTIAL OILS COLOR WHEEL
For quick reference, refer to our companion product, the Emotions and Essential Oils Wheel. One side lists negative emotions (what you would like less of in your life) and the other side lists positive properties (what you would like more of in your life). When you find the emotion or property that resonates with you, read the oil description in this book for a more complete understanding.

A COMPANION TO ESSENTIAL OIL REFERENCE BOOKS

This manual may also be used as a companion to essential oil reference books about physical health and application. After finding the recommended oils for your physical condition, cross-reference the oils with the emotional descriptions found in this book. For the most powerful results, choose the oils that match your emotional state as well as your physical condition.

SCANNING TECHNOLOGY

This book makes a great companion with scanning technologies that recommend an oil regimen for individuals to help with physical support, which can be used in conjunction with emotional healing.

SECTION II
SINGLE OILS

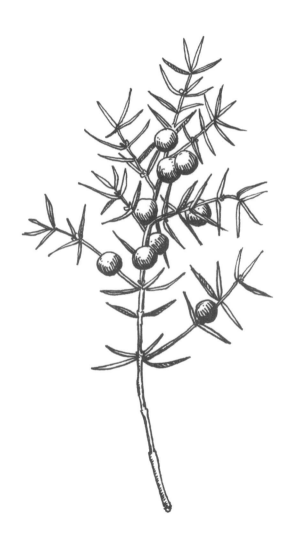

INTRODUCTION

In this section, we provide the core emotional properties of each essential oil, beginning with single oils and then oil blends. These descriptions briefly summarize the fruits of our research. The process for determining the focus of each oil includes gathering research on essential oils, such as their botanical and medicinal properties, plant family characteristics, history, and cultivation. The characteristics of each oil are also manifested through personal and professional use. In the final analysis, the representation of each oil has been guided and influenced by intuitive and energetic learning.

In each description, you will find the oil's emotional purpose summarized in the subtitle, which honors the emotional characteristics most prevalent in the oil. Both positive properties encouraged by the oil and the negative emotions addressed by the oil are listed, as well as a list of companion oils. The companion oils are provided to complement the primary properties of the oil. While the emotional stories of each individual are varied, we have offered complementary oils to support the core emotional state and provide alternatives for additional research and reflection.

We encourage you to read our book and decide if it resonates truth with you and will be of help in your healing journey. If so, we hope that you will hold space for these interpretations and recognize essential oils as powerful tools for emotional healing. It is our positive intention to offer support, clarity, and assistance to all those in need of healing, wherever they are on the path to wholeness.

ARBORVITAE
THE OIL OF DIVINE GRACE

Arborvitae assists individuals who believe or act like all progress must be made through struggle and solitary effort. Instead of trusting in the Divine, these individuals unconsciously block divine aid, choosing instead to live by their own efforts. Arborvitae addresses the need to control one's outcomes in life. It invites individuals to live with peace and joy by trusting in the abundant flow of divine grace.

Arborvitae is also a grounding oil that teaches Divinity is all around. God's grace can be felt and experienced here on earth; it is not distant or separate. God can help find balance in life and teach what to hold close and what to release.

Arborvitae's Latin name means "to sacrifice." This oil invites individuals to sacrifice their personal will and ambitions for a far more fulfilling way of living. By surrendering to God, the mind relaxes and the soul experiences harmony and peace. Arborvitae teaches that true strength can come through emptiness or a willingness to receive God's strength. It asks individuals to relax, take a deep breath, and trust in the flow of life. Arborvitae assists the soul to live effortlessly by divine grace.

NEGATIVE EMOTIONS: Willful, excessive effort, distrusting, rigid, fearful, controlling

POSITIVE PROPERTIES: Peaceful, surrender, grounded, trusting, relaxed, grace

COMPANION OILS: Basil, Cilantro, Oregano, Copaiba, Cumin

SUGGESTED USES:
Aromatic: Inhale from bottle, diffuse, or place drops in hand, rub, and inhale.

Topical: Apply 1-3 drops over solar plexus (upper stomach), on crown of head, or bottom of feet.

BASIL
THE OIL OF RENEWAL

The symptoms of adrenal exhaustion help identify the main moods that are improved with Basil, primarily fatigue, low energy, being overwhelmed, and the inability to cope with life's stressors. The smell of Basil oil brings strength to the heart and relaxation to the mind. This oil is also excellent for states of nervousness, anxiousness, and despair.

Basil oil supports those who are under a great deal of mental strain. It brings rejuvenation of vital forces after long periods of burnout and exhaustion. Basil oil may strengthen the adrenals and restore the body to its natural rhythms of sleep, activity, and rest.

Basil oil is also helpful for recovery from negative habits. It gives hope and optimism to the tired soul. Basil may assist an individual in giving up false stimulants or helping with substance abuse. By increasing natural energy, it helps individuals to achieve greater balance and health. In short, Basil is indicated for those who are weary in mind and body and for those in need of strength and renewal.

NEGATIVE EMOTIONS: Anxious, overwhelmed, drained, exhausted, negative habits

POSITIVE PROPERTIES: Energized, renewed, rejuvenated, rested, strengthened

COMPANION OILS: Wild Orange, Peppermint, Restful Blend, Grapefruit, Cumin, Digestive Blend, Red Mandarin, Tension Blends

SUGGESTED USES:
Aromatic: Inhale from bottle, diffuse, or place drops in hand, rub, and inhale.

Topical: Apply 3-5 drops over adrenal glands (lower back) or on bottom of feet in the morning and before bed.

BERGAMOT
THE OIL OF SELF-ACCEPTANCE

Bergamot relieves feelings of despair, self-judgment, and low self-esteem. It supports individuals in need of self-acceptance and self-love. Bergamot invites individuals to see life with more optimism.

Bergamot has a cleansing effect on stagnant feelings and limiting belief systems. Because of core beliefs of being bad, unlovable, and not good enough, they seek to hide behind a façade of cheerfulness. They may fear revealing their true thoughts and feelings. Bergamot's powerful cleansing properties generate movement in the energy system, which in turn brings hope.

In this way, Bergamot is wonderful for those who feel down and hopeless. It awakens the soul to hope and offers courage to share the inner self. Reigniting optimism and confidence in the self, it imparts true self-acceptance. Bergamot teaches individuals to let go of self-judgment by learning to love themselves unconditionally.

NEGATIVE EMOTIONS: Despairing, low self-esteem, self-judgment, unlovable, hopeless

POSITIVE PROPERTIES: Self-acceptance, optimistic, confident, hopeful, lovable, good enough

COMPANION OILS: Cassia, Metabolic Blend, Kumquat, Grapefruit, Copaiba

SUGGESTED USES:
Aromatic: Inhale from bottle or diffuse.

Topical: Dilute 1-3 drops with carrier oil and apply over heart, solar plexus (upper stomach), or on forehead.

BIRCH
THE OIL OF SUPPORT

Birch offers support to the unsupported. When a person is feeling attacked or unsupported in life, this oil offers courage to move forward alone. It helps individuals ground within their own center to find their source of inner support and strength. Learning to be flexible is important but so is gaining a strong backbone. Birch offers support to the weak-willed to stand tall and firm in what they believe, especially in situations where one is at risk of being rejected if they choose a different way. Birch lends its spirit of endurance to help individuals face trials of adversity, so they may weather storms with the strength and conviction of a tree.

Birch also encourages individuals to accept support when it is offered. Often, when individuals have carried their burdens alone, they don't know how to receive assistance. Birch counsels individuals to not become the reason they are unsupported, by blocking those who would lend their support. It reminds that it sometimes requires more strength to accept help than to go it alone.

Birch teaches those in need to trust that even if they are abandoned by all others, the Divine will always be there. It also reinforces there is more to life than pain, and with the right support and the right grounding, one can be held up and sustained through hardship.

NEGATIVE EMOTIONS: Unsupported, alienated, fearful, weak-willed, overly flexible, rejecting help

POSITIVE PROPERTIES: Supported, firm, resolute, strengthened, grounded, connected, receiving

COMPANION OILS: Cedarwood, White Fir, Coriander

SUGGESTED USES:
Aromatic: Inhale from bottle or diffuse.

Topical: Dilute 1-3 drops with carrier oil and apply along spine, over lower back, or on bottom of feet.

BLACK PEPPER

THE OIL OF UNMASKING

Black Pepper reveals the masks and façades used to hide aspects of the self. Since childhood, most individuals have been taught that some feelings and behaviors are good while others are not. So instead of seeking to understand seemingly inappropriate feelings and behaviors, they usually judge, condemn, and repress them. Individuals learn early on that to be loved and accepted, they must hide undesirable aspects of themselves behind a mask or façade.

Black Pepper invites individuals to get real by digging deep within the less understood parts of the self. Whether one's true motives and feelings are acknowledged or not, they continue to exist. The more these feelings are pushed down, buried, and repressed, the more they seek to make themselves known. If they are not honestly dealt with and acknowledged, they will often be expressed through erratic, compulsive, or addictive behaviors.

Black Pepper also reignites the soul fire, fueling motivation and high energy, and hastening the healing process. It gives individuals strength to overcome the challenges and issues they carry inside and invites them to live in integrity with their True Self.

NEGATIVE EMOTIONS: Emotional dishonesty, repressed emotions, trapped, prideful, superficial

POSITIVE PROPERTIES: Emotional honesty, authentic, courageous, motivated, self-aware, integrity

COMPANION OILS: Kumquat, Vetiver, Coriander, Juniper Berry, Frankincense

SUGGESTED USES:
Aromatic: Inhale from bottle or diffuse.

Topical: Dilute 1-2 drops with carrier oil and apply on bottom of feet.

BLUE TANSY
THE OIL OF INSPIRED ACTION

Blue Tansy supports those who resist taking action to change or transform their circumstances. It is especially helpful when individuals have become stagnant in their progression. It provides a kind of catalytic spark that overcomes the tendency to vacillate, avoid, or procrastinate. Blue Tansy necessitates that individuals choose to take the helm of their life. It also encourages individuals to live in alignment with the whisperings of their inner voice, prompting them to make necessary changes. When an individual represses these messages, they often feel lethargic, drained, apathetic, sluggish, and exhausted. Blue Tansy invites individuals to take the initiative to reclaim the life they dream of.

Blue Tansy invites individuals to manifest their passion into action. This is especially important when there is a desire to retreat or self-sabotage. By creating more inward mobility, Blue Tansy encourages them to accept all that is, including emotional setbacks and other challenges which must be overcome to actualize inspiration and sustain change. Blue Tansy teaches that each act is based on choice and requires individuals to own the responsibility of their cumulative choices. It demands personal mastery and purposeful action in achieving one's fullest potential.

NEGATIVE EMOTIONS: Procrastinating, resisting change and inner guidance, uninspired, exhausted, lethargic, apathetic, self-sabotage

POSITIVE PROPERTIES: Inspired, initiative, committed, responsive, energized, motivated, purposeful, responsible

COMPANION OILS: Litsea, Coriander, Roman Chamomile, Fennel

SUGGESTED USES:
Aromatic: Inhale from bottle or diffuse.

Topical: Dilute 1-3 drops with carrier oil and apply behind ears, on wrists, over solar plexus (upper stomach), or on bottom of feet.

CARDAMOM
THE OIL OF OBJECTIVITY

Cardamom helps individuals to regain objectivity, mental sobriety, and self-control. It assists individuals who frequently feel frustrated or angry with other people. Cardamom is especially helpful for times when one's anger goes to their head, causing them to become hotheaded. In such situations, the individual becomes inebriated with anger, losing control and rational function. Cardamom helps to bring balance, mental clarity, and objectivity during moments of extreme anger and frustration.

Cardamom is especially beneficial for individuals with a long history of anger or aggression, which often becomes directed outward. It is helpful for those who hyperfocus on their problems, especially their frustrations. Cardamom assists individuals in breaking down or digesting these intense emotions of frustration and anger by redirecting energy to the solar plexus, the center of responsibility. In this way, Cardamom helps individuals let go of emotional distortions which cause them to objectify other people and see them as inconveniences.

Cardamom demands that individuals stop blaming others. It asks them to take personal ownership and responsibility for their feelings. As they do, they will feel more at peace, calm, and in control of themselves.

NEGATIVE EMOTIONS: Inebriated by anger, easily frustrated, objectifying others, blaming, unable to think clearly

POSITIVE PROPERTIES: Objective, self-control, respectful, tolerant, patient, mental sobriety

COMPANION OILS: Thyme, Restful Blend, Oregano

SUGGESTED USES:
Aromatic: Inhale from bottle or diffuse.

Topical: Dilute 1-2 drops with carrier oil and apply anywhere anger is held in the body.

CASSIA
THE OIL OF SELF-ASSURANCE

Cassia brings gladness and courage to the heart and soul. It is a wonderful remedy for the shy and timid. It helps those who hold back and try to hide. When a person avoids being the center of attention, Cassia can restore their confidence.

Similar to Cinnamon, Cassia dispels fear and replaces it with self-assurance. It challenges individuals to try, even when they are afraid of making mistakes. Cassia aids those who feel foolish by helping them see their own brilliance. It supports the soul in seeing its own value and potential. Cassia assists individuals in discovering their innate gifts and talents. It invites them to let their light shine and live from their True Self.

NEGATIVE EMOTIONS: Embarrassed, hiding, fearful, humiliated, insecure, judged, shy, worthless

POSITIVE PROPERTIES: Courageous, self-assured, unashamed, confident, valued, authentic

COMPANION OILS: Spearmint, Clove, Roman Chamomile, Litsea

SUGGESTED USES:
Aromatic: Inhale from bottle or diffuse.

Topical: Dilute 1 drop or less with carrier oil and apply over solar plexus (upper stomach) or on bottom of feet.

NOTE: Cassia can be irritating to skin; be cautious when using topically.

CEDARWOOD
THE OIL OF COMMUNITY

Cedarwood brings people together to experience the strength and value of community. Those in need of Cedarwood struggle to form bonds within social groups. This can often be due to an overdeveloped sense of individuality. Rather than allowing themselves to be supported by family, friends, or a community, they live by excessive self-reliance. On the other hand, the individual's difficulty forming social roots may also stem from feeling disconnected and separate from the human family. Cedarwood inspires the feeling of belonging and assists the heart in opening to receive the love and support of other people. It invites the strong-willed individual to couple the strength of individuality with the supportive power of community.

Cedarwood supports individuals in seeing that they are not alone; life is a shared experience. Cedarwood also assists in opening the awareness of individuals to the support system that is already available to them, such as friends or family that have been overlooked. It invites individuals to both give and receive, so they may experience the strength of groups and the joy of relationships.

NEGATIVE EMOTIONS: Inability to form social bonds, lonely, feeling separate from the human family, antisocial

POSITIVE PROPERTIES: Emotionally connected, belonging, supported, social bonds, sociable, community oriented

COMPANION OILS: Marjoram, Birch

SUGGESTED USES:
Aromatic: Inhale from bottle or diffuse.

Topical: Dilute 3-4 drops with carrier oil and apply on arms, legs, or bottom of feet.

CILANTRO
THE OIL OF RELEASING CONTROL

Cilantro facilitates a detoxification of negative emotions and debris. It is helpful in lightening one's load through the release of issues buried in the body, heart, and soul. Similar to Coriander oil, which is distilled from the seeds of the same plant, Cilantro assists individuals in shedding what is not in harmony with their True Self.

Those in need of Cilantro may attempt to obsessively control other people or manage their environment. Inwardly, these individuals may experience a great deal of worry and mental strain. They may become constricted, clinging to or obsessing over material possessions. Individuals may even hold onto the very patterns, emotions, issues, and possessions that may impair or betray their True Self.

Cilantro facilitates emotional cleansing, and especially encourages the release of worry and control as it assists individuals in centering in their True Self. Cilantro liberates the soul from heavy burdens, enabling the individual to live light and free.

NEGATIVE EMOTIONS: Controlling, toxic, constricted, obsessive-compulsive, clingy, worried, trapped

POSITIVE PROPERTIES: Cleansing, liberated, detached, untroubled

COMPANION OILS: Wintergreen, Cypress, Cinnamon, Reassuring Blend, Cardamom

SUGGESTED USES:
Aromatic: Inhale from bottle, diffuse, or place drops in hand, rub, and inhale.

Topical: Apply 1-3 drops over throat or solar plexus (upper stomach).

CINNAMON

THE OIL OF SEXUAL HARMONY

Cinnamon strongly supports the reproductive system and helps heal sexual issues. It assists individuals in accepting their body and embracing their physical attractiveness. Cinnamon dispels fear of rejection and nurtures healthy sexuality. It rekindles sexual energies when there has been repression, trauma, or abuse. It can also bring clarity to souls who struggle with their sexual identity.

Cinnamon also assists individuals in relationships where insecurities are shown by jealousy or control. It encourages the soul to let go of control and allow others to be free. Cinnamon can nurture strong relationships based on mutual love and respect. Where there are other insecurities covered by pretense, façade, and pride, Cinnamon invites individuals to be honest and vulnerable, thereby allowing true intimacy to emerge.

NEGATIVE EMOTIONS: Body shame, fearful, controlling, jealous, sexual abuse, sexual repression or overactive sexuality

POSITIVE PROPERTIES: Body acceptance, attractive, accepted, healthy sexuality, intimate

COMPANION OILS: Jasmine, Bergamot, Grapefruit, Neroli

SUGGESTED USES:
Aromatic: Inhale from bottle or diffuse.

Topical: Dilute 1 drop or less with carrier oil and apply over sacral chakra (lower stomach).

NOTE: Cinnamon can be irritating to skin; be cautious when using topically.

CLARY SAGE
THE OIL OF CLARITY & VISION

Clary Sage assists individuals in changing their perceptions. It gives courage to see the truth. One of the finest oils for the brow chakra, Clary Sage dispels darkness and illusion, helping individuals to see their limiting belief systems. Clary Sage encourages individuals to remain open to new ideas and new perspectives. It can assist during a healing crisis when a drastic change of perspective is required. Clary Sage opens the soul to new possibilities and experiences.

Clary Sage assists in opening creative channels and clearing creative blocks. It eliminates distractions from the mind and assists individuals in finding a state of emptiness where creative forces may be realized. Opening individuals to the dream world, Clary Sage increases the ability to visualize and imagine new possibilities.

Clary Sage teaches the spirit how to use its divinely given gifts and is especially helpful in clarifying spiritual vision. It assists in developing the gift of discernment. Clary Sage invites individuals to expand their vision and accept the reality of the spiritual world.

NEGATIVE EMOTIONS: Confused, darkness, spiritually disconnected, hopeless, blocked creativity

POSITIVE PROPERTIES: Spiritual clarity, intuitive, open-minded, imaginative, spiritually discerning

COMPANION OILS: Lemongrass, Black Pepper, Juniper Berry, Rosemary, Melissa

SUGGESTED USES:
Aromatic: Inhale from bottle, diffuse, or place drops in hand, rub, and inhale.

Topical: Apply 1-2 drops on forehead or behind ears.

CLOVE

THE OIL OF BOUNDARIES

Clove supports individuals in letting go of victim mentality. Victims feel overly influenced by other people and outside circumstances. They perceive themselves as powerless to change their life situations. Clove helps individuals stand up for themselves, be proactive, and feel capable of making their own choices, regardless of others.

Clove assists individuals in letting go of patterns of self-betrayal and codependency by reconnecting them with their personal integrity. It builds up appropriate boundaries and defenses. Clove gives pushovers the courage to say "no." It reignites the soul fire and can assist anytime there has been damage related to childhood pain, trauma, or abuse. Clove is helpful for breaking free of patterns of abuse by restoring the victim's sense of self and helping them regain strength to stand up for their needs. Clove insists that individuals live true to themselves and the Divine by establishing clear boundaries.

NEGATIVE EMOTIONS: Victim mentality, defeated, dominated, enslaved, fear of rejection, intimidated, controlled, codependent

POSITIVE PROPERTIES: Empowered, clear boundaries, protected, courageous, independent, capable, proactive, integrity

COMPANION OILS: Ginger, Helichrysum, Melaleuca, Coriander

SUGGESTED USES:
Aromatic: Inhale from bottle or diffuse.

Topical: Dilute 1 drop or less with carrier oil and apply on bottom of feet or over sacral chakra (lower stomach).

> **NOTE:** Clove can be irritating to skin; be cautious when using topically.

COPAIBA
THE OIL OF UNVEILING

Copaiba invites individuals to connect with their past. It offers a deep intertwining energy that links experience to experience to unveil the deeper meaning and messages showing up in one's life. Copaiba respects the sacred sheltered within until it is ready to emerge into the light of consciousness. It then invites individuals to become thoughtfully aware of the shadow aspects of themselves and discover who they really are.

Individuals in need of Copaiba often find that vulnerable self-awareness work reveals unresolved pain in hidden recesses of their heart, mind, and body. Many discover they are plagued with feelings of guilt, shame, inadequacy, or unworthiness that have been absorbed from their early environment. These shame-based feelings distort every interaction they have with life. Everything seen through the filter of "less than" creates a perception of the world that is extremely painful and ultimately defeating. Copaiba offers assistance to those caught in lower vibrations of shame, blame, fear, and self-loathing, and other unconsciously internalized emotions. It summons them to begin the unraveling and restoration process necessary for lasting healing and further awareness and insight.

Copaiba invites those who have done something that causes guilt or shame to undergo appropriate remorse and then move on, remembering that forgiveness of the self is also necessary. If not dealt with, these lowest vibrational emotions will drive an individual to rebel or overcompensate. Both are a product of running from their center of truth and existence. Acknowledging the reality of past choices and experiences allows individuals to grow and change in more conscious and clear ways.

Copaiba also invites individuals to come to the Divine for clarity and redefinition. It reminds that the Divine knows them anciently as whole beings—from their earliest childhood wounds to their current limitations. The Divine, as the source and connecting force of everything, possesses the wisdom that transcends mortal perception. Copaiba reassures that mental, emotional, physical, and spiritual limitations are only temporary. The Divine does not expect individuals to navigate the challenges of life alone or avoid the things they need to experience in life to produce necessary growth and change. Instead, Copaiba teaches that the Divine will reveal the higher message of one's life. It will unveil that they have always been treasured, accepted, valued, worthy of love, and much more. Copaiba imparts that it is only through this divine unveiling that individuals can fully accept the magnificence of what they really are and make peace with the past.

NEGATIVE EMOTIONS: Shameful, guilty, regretful, self-loathing, less than, unworthy, suppressed emotions, rebelling

POSITIVE PROPERTIES: Worthy, self-aware, clarity, forgiven, redefinition of self, purposeful existence

COMPANION OILS: Helichrysum, Frankincense, Black Pepper, Renewing Blend, Topical Blend

SUGGESTED USES:
Aromatic: Inhale from bottle, diffuse, or place drops in hand, rub, and inhale.

Topical: Apply 1-3 drops over heart, sacral chakra (lower stomach), on forehead, crown of head, or nape of neck.

CORIANDER
THE OIL OF INTEGRITY

Coriander is the oil of integrity, specifically integrity with oneself. The person in need of Coriander oil may be trapped in a cycle of serving others while neglecting their own needs. They may also have a strong desire to do what is right or correct. Often the mind's perspective of the right way is too limited when seen from only one perspective. Coriander reminds individuals that there is more than one way to do something, and that fitting in often requires betraying the True Self.

Coriander moves the individual from doing things for the acceptance of others to honoring and living from the True Self. There are as many ways of being as there are people in the world. Each soul must learn its own way of living and being. Coriander gives courage to step out of the box and risk being who one really is.

Coriander teaches that each individual is a gift to the world with something unique, which no one else has to offer. Only they can express their uniqueness. Integrity with oneself means living in connection with what one's spirit urges and directs. Coriander helps individuals live from the True Self.

NEGATIVE EMOTIONS: Controlled by others, self-betrayal, drudgery, conforming

POSITIVE PROPERTIES: True to self, inner guidance, integrity, unique

COMPANION OILS: Roman Chamomile, Ginger, Kumquat

SUGGESTED USES:
Aromatic: Inhale from bottle, diffuse, or place drops in hand, rub, and inhale.

Topical: Apply 1-3 drops over solar plexus (upper stomach) or on bottom of feet.

CUMIN
THE OIL OF BALANCED AMBITION

Cumin essential oil is a balancing force for personal will and ambition. Cumin teaches that while motivation and drive can be powerful catalysts for change, individuals lose integrity when that ambition comes at the expense of others. Often, individuals allow their attachment to a desired outcome to eclipse the needs and feelings of those in their family or social group. They can falsely believe that their enthusiasm for their personal desires or goals make up for inconveniences and insensitivities imposed on others. Cumin addresses this imbalance in relationships, inviting individuals to surrender their unbridled ambition and attachment to outcomes, focusing instead on cooperation and consideration of others.

While cultural norms often teach that success in life is a determinant of happiness, Cumin oil reminds that meaningful relationships have a more direct impact on overall happiness and life satisfaction. This oil warns that when one's drive to reach the top is at the expense of others, they arrive alone.

Cumin also encourages individuals who struggle with a self-centered existence to dig deeper into what is causing these behaviors. Individuals often find the underlying cause may be fear of failure, not being important, not being valued, or not having enough. Cumin eases the anxiousness of these deeper emotional states, encouraging healing from within. It also invites individuals to address the scarcity mindset that drives them to over-impose their will. Additionally, Cumin encourages the positive aspects of zeal that come from feeling secure, respectful, valuable, and energized, without being overbearing. It teaches that healthy zeal comes from knowing why individuals pursue their course and helps them feel confident to accomplish their life mission and goals.

NEGATIVE EMOTIONS: Overly ambitious, insensitive, attachment to outcomes, self-centered, fear of failure, scarcity mindset

POSITIVE PROPERTIES: Balanced zeal, considerate, respectful, nonattachment to success, abundant thinking

COMPANION OILS: Oregano, Wild Orange, Lemongrass, Spikenard, Coriander, Basil

SUGGESTED USES:
Aromatic: Inhale from a bottle or diffuse.

Topical: Dilute 1 drop or less with carrier oil and apply over solar plexus (upper stomach) or on bottom of feet.

> **NOTE:** Cumin can be irritating to skin; be cautious when using topically.

CYPRESS
THE OIL OF MOTION & FLOW

This powerful oil creates energetic flow and emotional catharsis. Stagnant energies are brought into motion through the fluid energy of this oil. Cypress works in the heart and mind, creating flexibility.

Cypress teaches the soul how to let go of the past by moving with the flow of life. This oil is especially indicated for individuals who are mentally or emotionally stuck, stiff, rigid, tense, overstriving, or have perfectionistic tendencies. This hard driving stems from fear and the need to control. The individual tries to force things in life rather than allowing them to unfold naturally.

Cypress encourages individuals to cast aside their worries and let go of control so they can enjoy the thrill that comes from being alive. It reminds individuals that damnation is simply the discontinuation of growth and development, and invites them to step out of the way and allow life to flow freely or without compulsion. Cypress shows how to have perfect trust in the flow of life.

NEGATIVE EMOTIONS: Controlling, fearful, perfectionistic, rigid, stuck, tense

POSITIVE PROPERTIES: Flexible, trusting, flowing with life, adaptable

COMPANION OILS: Wintergreen, Cilantro, Thyme, Massage Blend

SUGGESTED USES:
Aromatic: Inhale from bottle, diffuse, or place drops in hand, rub, and inhale.

Topical: Apply 1-3 drops along spine or on bottom of feet.

DILL
THE OIL OF LEARNING

Dill supports individuals in learning new things, thinking rationally, and integrating different thoughts into coherent ideas.

This oil is especially helpful for those who feel despondent, bored, or disinterested in the learning process. It supports those who have a difficult time engaging, especially in the classroom. Dill is helpful for those individuals who may feel overwhelmed by too many ideas or by too much stimulus in their environment. Dill can assist individuals to digest and integrate all this information. It supports the left and right brain in working together harmoniously. It can also assist individuals in overcoming mental sluggishness by encouraging awake, alert involvement.

Dill encourages individuals to embrace the many facets of life by engaging in the learning process. It challenges individuals to become self-motivated learners and to find excitement for discovering new things. It assists individuals in assimilating different thoughts and ideas.

NEGATIVE EMOTIONS: Bored, disinterested, disengaged, overstimulated

POSITIVE PROPERTIES: Engaged, motivated, integration, mental clarity

COMPANION OILS: Rosemary, Lemon, Digestive Blend

SUGGESTED USES:
Aromatic: Inhale from bottle, diffuse, or place drops in hand, rub, and inhale.

Topical: Apply 1-3 drops on nape of neck or over solar plexus (upper stomach).

DOUGLAS FIR

THE OIL OF GENERATIONAL WISDOM

Douglas Fir and White Fir share many similar qualities; however Douglas firs live a longer life and would be considered the older and wiser of the two trees. They both address generational issues by inviting individuals to break free from destructive traditions passed down through their families. Like White Fir, Douglas Fir assists individuals to live according to their own conscience and values by letting go of harmful patterns. It teaches that each generation can be a gift of new life, new growth, and new beginnings. Similarly, Douglas Fir can also assist with increasing the bond within one's family. It encourages healthy family dynamics where people and meaningful relationships are valued over blind loyalty to traditions.

Additionally, Douglas Fir teaches individuals to learn from and value others' experiences, especially one's family and ancestors. It encourages respect for one's elders and ancestral heritage. Douglas Fir reminds individuals that valuable wisdom can be obtained by learning from the past, especially from individuals who are older, wiser, and more experienced.

NEGATIVE EMOTIONS: Negative generational patterns, burdened by family issues

POSITIVE PROPERTIES: Generational healing, respect for elders, wisdom, learning from the past

COMPANION OILS: White Fir, Petitgrain

SUGGESTED USES:
Aromatic: Inhale from bottle, diffuse, or place drops in hand, rub, and inhale.

Topical: Apply 1-3 drops on base of spine or on bottom of feet.

EUCALYPTUS

THE OIL OF WELLNESS

The strong medicinal aroma of Eucalyptus demonstrates its powerful effect upon the physical and emotional bodies. Eucalyptus oil supports the soul who is constantly facing illness. They may get well for times and seasons, only to return to a common cold, allergies, or congestion in the sinuses and respiratory system.

Eucalyptus addresses a deep emotional or spiritual issue of the need to be sick. It reveals patterns of thinking that continually create poor health. These beliefs may include thoughts such as "I don't deserve to be well," "I am the sort of person that is always getting sick," or "The only way I can get a break is to get sick." Eucalyptus gives individuals courage to face these issues and beliefs. It encourages them to let go of their attachments to illness.

Eucalyptus encourages individuals to take full responsibility for their own health. It bestows trust that one's needs and desires can be met, even if they allow themselves to be well. Eucalyptus teaches how to claim wholeness and heal.

NEGATIVE EMOTIONS: Attached to illness, clingy, defeated, despairing, desire to escape life or responsibilities, imprisoned, powerless to heal

POSITIVE PROPERTIES: Able to heal, well, liberated, responsible, encouraged

COMPANION OILS: Respiratory Blend, Fennel, Lime, Patchouli, Spikenard

SUGGESTED USES:
Aromatic: Inhale from bottle or diffuse.

Topical: Dilute 2-4 drops with carrier oil and apply over lungs, chest, or throat.

FENNEL
THE OIL OF RESPONSIBILITY

Fennel supports the individual who has a weakened sense of self. The individual may feel defeated by life's responsibilities, having little or no desire to improve their situation. Fennel reignites a passion for life. It encourages the soul to take full ownership and responsibility for its choices. Fennel teaches that life is not too much or too big to handle.

Fennel encourages individuals to live in integrity with themselves, despite the judgments of others. When they have been paralyzed by fear and shame, this oil gets them moving again. Fennel reestablishes a strong connection to the body and the self when there has been weakness or separation.

Fennel also supports an individual in listening to the subtle messages of the body. This is especially important in situations where there has been a loss of connection to the body's natural signals due to emotional eating, severe dieting, eating issues, or drug abuse. Through attunement with the body's actual needs, Fennel curbs cravings for experiences that dull the senses. This oil then supports the individual in hearing the body's signals of hunger, thirst, satiation, or exhaustion. Fennel is also supportive in regaining one's appetite for nourishment, food, and life itself.

NEGATIVE EMOTIONS: Lack of desire, unwilling to take responsibility, shameful, weak sense of self, numb to body signals

POSITIVE PROPERTIES: Responsible, in tune with body, satiated

COMPANION OILS: Ginger, Tangerine, Grapefruit, Patchouli, Blue Tansy, Eucalyptus

SUGGESTED USES:
Aromatic: Inhale from bottle or diffuse.

Topical: Dilute 1-3 drops with carrier oil and apply over entire stomach before or after meals.

FRANKINCENSE
THE OIL OF TRUTH

Frankincense reveals deceptions and false truths. It invites individuals to let go of lower vibrations, lies, deceptions, and negativity. This oil helps create new perspectives based on light and truth. Frankincense recalls to memory spiritual understanding, gifts, wisdom, and knowledge that the soul brought into the world. It is a powerful cleanser of spiritual darkness. Frankincense assists in pulling the "scales of darkness" from the eyes, the barriers from the mind, and the walls from the heart. Through connecting the soul with its inner light, this oil reveals the truth.

Frankincense supports in creating a healthy attachment with one's father. It assists in spiritual awakening and helps an individual feel the love of the Divine. When one has felt abandoned or forgotten, Frankincense reminds them that they are loved and protected. While this oil is incredibly powerful, it is also gentle, like a loving father who nurtures, guides, and protects. Frankincense shields the body and soul from negative influences and assists the soul in its spiritual evolution. Enhancing practices of prayer and meditation, this oil opens spiritual channels that allow an individual to connect to God. Through the light and power of Frankincense, the individual can draw closer to divinity, healthy masculinity, and the grandeur of the True Self.

NEGATIVE EMOTIONS: Abandoned, spiritually disconnected, distant from father, unprotected, spiritual darkness

POSITIVE PROPERTIES: Enlightened, loved, protected, wisdom, discerning, spiritually open, connected to father

COMPANION OILS: Melissa, Manuka, Myrrh, Litsea, Roman Chamomile

SUGGESTED USES:

Aromatic: Inhale from bottle, diffuse, or place drops in hand, rub, and inhale.

Topical: Apply 1-3 drops on crown of head, forehead, or behind ears.

Environment: Add several drops into spray bottle and mist around home.

GERANIUM
THE OIL OF LOVE & TRUST

Geranium restores confidence in the innate goodness of others and in the world. It facilitates trust, especially when individuals have lost trust in others due to difficult life circumstances. It also assists in reestablishing a strong bond to one's mother and father. When there has been a loss of trust in relationships, Geranium encourages emotional honesty, love, and forgiveness. It fosters receptivity to human love and connection.

Geranium aids in healing the broken heart. It encourages emotional honesty by facilitating the emergence of grief or pain that has been suppressed. Geranium softens anger and assists in healing emotional wounds. It assists in reopening the heart so that love may flow freely. Indeed, Geranium could be called "the emotional healer."

Geranium is a gentle oil, perfect for babies and children. It nurtures the inner child and supports in re-parenting this aspect of the self. Individuals who have a difficult time accessing their emotions can be supported by Geranium, as it leads away from the logical mind and into the warmth and nurture of the heart. At its root, Geranium heals the heart, instills unconditional love, and fosters trust.

NEGATIVE EMOTIONS: Abandoned, loss, distrusting, unforgiving, unloving, disheartened, heavyhearted, grieving

POSITIVE PROPERTIES: Emotional healing, empathetic, trusting, forgiving, gentle, loving, tolerant, open

COMPANION OILS: Copaiba, Manuka, Marjoram, Neroli, Ylang Ylang, Rose, Renewing Blend

SUGGESTED USES:
Aromatic: Inhale from bottle or diffuse.

Topical: Dilute 1-3 drops with carrier oil and apply over heart.

GINGER
THE OIL OF EMPOWERMENT

Ginger holds no reservations. This oil has a purpose and will fulfill it! Ginger powerfully persuades individuals to be fully present and participate in life. It teaches that to be successful in life, one must be wholly committed to it.

Ginger addresses deep patterns of victim mentality, which is evidenced by feelings of powerlessness, believing everything is outside one's control, refusing to take responsibility for life, or blaming life circumstances on other people or outside influences. Victims feel stuck as they decentralize or disown responsibility and blame others for their misfortunes.

Ginger empowers individuals in taking complete responsibility for their life circumstances. It infuses a warrior-like mentality based on integrity, personal responsibility, and individual choice. Here, individuals see themselves as the creators of their own lives. No longer waiting for outside circumstances to change, they choose their own destiny. The empowered individuals assume full responsibility and accountability for the consequences of their actions or inactions.

NEGATIVE EMOTIONS: Victim mentality, powerless, unwilling to take responsibility, defeated, not present, stuck, blaming others

POSITIVE PROPERTIES: Empowered, committed, capable, purposeful, accountable

COMPANION OILS: Cassia, Fennel, Blue Tansy, Encouraging Blend, Inspiring Blend, Spearmint

SUGGESTED USES:
Aromatic: Inhale from bottle or diffuse.

Topical: Dilute 1-2 drops with carrier oil and apply over solar plexus (upper stomach).

GRAPEFRUIT
THE OIL OF HONORING THE BODY

Grapefruit teaches true respect and appreciation for one's physical body. It supports individuals who struggle to honor their body and are caught in patterns of mistreatment. These forms of abuse may include severe dieting, judging one's body weight or type, and abusing the body through negligent behavior or violence. These acts are often motivated by hate and disgust buried within the psyche, which gets directed toward the physical body. Though individuals may obsess over how they look, deep down they never feel they look good enough. There is a dissatisfaction that persists.

Grapefruit oil is often misused in overly strict dietary and weight-loss programs. The reason this oil helps curb emotional eating is because it encourages a positive relationship with one's body based on love, tolerance, and acceptance. Grapefruit encourages integrity by respecting one's physical needs. This oil assists individuals in listening to their true physical needs and impulses. It also assists them in taking responsibility for what they feel. Grapefruit teaches that no amount of food can fill a hole in the heart—only love can do that. As individuals take ownership of their feelings and get the help they need in addressing them, they no longer have a need to hide their feelings behind food, body abuse, strict regimens, eating issues, or other forms of obsession.

NEGATIVE EMOTIONS: Body shame, obsession with food or dieting, eating issues, distorted self-image, hiding

POSITIVE PROPERTIES: Respectful of physical needs, body acceptance, nourished, healthy relationship with food

COMPANION OILS: Patchouli, Bergamot, Metabolic Blend, Fennel

SUGGESTED USES:
Aromatic: Inhale from bottle, diffuse, or place drops in hand, rub, and inhale.

Topical: Apply 1-3 drops on wrists or over entire stomach.

HELICHRYSUM
THE OIL FOR PAIN

Helichrysum is an amazing healer of pain. It aids the walking wounded—those with a history of difficult life circumstances, trauma, self-destruction, loss, or abuse. These individuals need the powerful spiritual support that Helichrysum offers. It gives strength and endurance to the wounded soul who must keep on living, despite past difficulties. This oil restores confidence in life and in the self, giving the individual strength to carry on. Helichrysum has a powerful relationship with the light of the sun. It imbues joy, fervor, and hope for living. Helichrysum takes hurt souls by the hand, guiding them through life's difficulties. If individuals can persevere, this oil can take them into new heights of spiritual consciousness. Helichrysum offers hope that wounds can be healed.

Following this spiritual healing and transformation, Helichrysum can teach individuals to have gratitude for their trials. It helps them to see that if they had not been wounded, they would not have sought healing that resulted in a spiritual rebirth. Just as the phoenix dies and rises from its ashes, so might an individual be raised from turmoil. Helichrysum lends its warrior spirit so that one may face adversities with courage and determination. It brings hope to the most discouraged of souls and life to those in need of rebirth.

NEGATIVE EMOTIONS: Intense emotional pain, anguish, or trauma; hopeless, despairing, wounded

POSITIVE PROPERTIES: Healing, courageous, hopeful, transforming, persevering, determined

COMPANION OILS: Hope Blend, Soothing Blend, Ginger, Wintergreen, Lime, Siberian Fir, Peppermint

SUGGESTED USES:
Aromatic: Inhale from bottle, diffuse, or place drops in hand, rub, and inhale.

Topical: Apply 1-3 drops over heart or wherever pain is experienced.

JASMINE
THE OIL OF SEXUAL PURITY & BALANCE

Jasmine nurtures healthy sexuality and helps to balance sexual forces. It may also arouse dormant passions, assisting individuals to regain interest in the sexual experience. Jasmine cultivates positive experiences within intimate relationships by encouraging the purification of unhealthy sexual intentions and motivations. It asks individuals to honor and respect themselves and others.

Jasmine encourages the release of past sexual trauma. Through its gentle, purifying nature, Jasmine brings forward unresolved sexual experiences and facilitates the healing process. Traumatic experiences can distort one's relationship with sexuality. Jasmine can assist both kinds of common compensations: those who fear, repel, or resist the sexual experience, as well as those who obsess over or are fixated on sexuality. It is balancing for individuals who use sex to fill a desperate need for love and approval, as well as individuals who resist sexual intimacy.

Jasmine supports the resolution of sexual trauma, encourages safety within intimate relationships, and invites only the purest intentions to the sexual experience.

NEGATIVE EMOTIONS: Unresolved sexual trauma, sexual repression, sexual fixation

POSITIVE PROPERTIES: Healthy sexuality, pure intentions, innocent, healing, self-acceptance, intimate, trust, safe

COMPANION OILS: Cinnamon, Neroli

SUGGESTED USES:
Aromatic: Inhale from bottle, diffuse, or place drops in hand, rub, and inhale.

Topical: Apply 1-2 drops over sacral chakra (lower stomach), lower back, or behind ears.

JUNIPER BERRY

THE OIL OF NIGHT

Juniper Berry assists those who fear the dark or unknown aspects of themselves. It helps individuals to understand that those things they fear are intended to be their teachers. Instead of hiding from what they do not understand, Juniper Berry encourages individuals to learn the lesson and face their fear. These fears often live within the unexplored areas of the self. Juniper Berry acts as a catalyst by helping individuals access and address those fears and issues which have long been avoided.

Dreams contain nighttime communications. Even nightmares can reveal unresolved fears and issues. Juniper Berry offers courage and energetic protection in the nighttime. It encourages an honest assessment of the information being communicated from within. As individuals reconcile with their fears and other hidden aspects of themselves, they experience greater wholeness. Juniper Berry helps restore the balance between light and dark, conscious and subconscious, day and night. It acts as a guide on the path toward wholeness. Juniper Berry teaches that there is truly nothing to fear when one acknowledges and accepts all aspects of the self.

NEGATIVE EMOTIONS: Irrational fears, recurrent nightmares, disrupted sleep, avoiding

POSITIVE PROPERTIES: Protected, peaceful dreaming, courageous, self-aware

COMPANION OILS: Black Pepper, Clary Sage, Protective Blend, Vetiver

SUGGESTED USES:
Aromatic: Inhale from bottle, diffuse, or place drops in hand, rub, and inhale before bed.

Topical: Apply 1 drop on forehead or behind ears before bed.

Environment: Add several drops into spray bottle and mist around bedroom.

KUMQUAT OIL
THE OIL OF AUTHENTIC PRESENCE

Kumquats are unique in the citrus family with the sweetest part of the fruit contained on the outside, in the peel. The complexity of complementary flavors lies within. As such, Kumquat oil addresses preoccupation with a cheerful external disposition that masks anxiousness, self-doubt, pain, and unease hidden within.

Individuals in need of Kumquat oil tend to judge and push down feelings deemed as unacceptable or unwanted. Often they have been taught to repress feelings in order to be accepted. These personalities appear happy, enthusiastic, popular, and seemingly at peace in the world while their inner torment is meticulously guarded and hidden from view. However, this denial, avoidance of emotional pain, and fear of negative emotions can lead to destructive coping strategies and passive aggressiveness in order to continue keeping up the chosen façade.

Kumquat oil instructs that true happiness comes only through real, honest, and unstudied living. It reminds that people are a complement of good and bad, sweet and sour. Individuals must embrace their multifaceted humanness and anchor their identity in the truth in order to live authentically. Kumquat invites all to shift their focus away from outward behaviors or pretenses—which others may validate—and instead begin the quiet, consistent, and unseen journey to inner alignment, contentment, and healing.

NEGATIVE EMOTIONS: Superficial, façade of cheerfulness, hiding, inauthentic, repressed feelings, passive aggressive

POSITIVE PROPERTIES: Unstudied, authentic, real, honest, sincere, unpretentious, aligned

COMPANION OILS: Black Pepper, Coriander, Lavender

SUGGESTED USES:

Aromatic: Inhale from bottle, diffuse, or place drops in hand, rub, and inhale

Topical: Apply 1-3 drops over throat, stomach, or forehead.

LAVENDER
THE OIL OF COMMUNICATION & CALM

Lavender aids verbal expression and calming the mind. Specifically, it calms the insecurities that are felt when one risks their true thoughts and feelings. Lavender addresses a deep fear of being seen and heard. Individuals in need of Lavender hide within, blocking their true self-expression. While they may be going through the motions of outward expression, they're actually holding back their innermost thoughts and feelings. The expression is not connected to the heart or soul.

Lavender supports individuals in releasing the tension and constriction that stems from withheld expression. This bottleneck in communication can result in worried and racing thoughts, anxiousness, and sleep disruption. Due to past experiences, they may feel unsafe or fearful of expressing themselves because of potential rejection. Often they don't allow themselves space to get in touch with all they truly think and feel. Their true voice is therefore trapped within and goes unexpressed. Strong feelings of being unlovable, unimportant, or unheard can accompany this condition.

Lavender encourages emotional honesty and insists that one speak their innermost thoughts and desires. As individuals learn to communicate their deepest thoughts and feelings, they are liberated from their self-inflicted prison. It is through open and honest communication that an individual has the potential to experience unconditional love, acceptance, and peace of mind. Through Lavender's courageous spirit, one is free to share their True Self with others.

NEGATIVE EMOTIONS: Blocked communication, fear of rejection, constricted, tense, racing thoughts, emotional dishonesty, hiding, fear of self-disclosure; feeling unseen, unheard, or unloved

POSITIVE PROPERTIES: Open communication, calm, expressive, emotional honesty, self-aware, peace of mind

COMPANION OILS: Spearmint, Restful Blend

SUGGESTED USES:

Aromatic: Inhale from bottle, diffuse, or place drops in hand, rub, and inhale.

Topical: Apply 1-3 drops over throat, temples, or on nape of neck.

LEMON
THE OIL OF FOCUS

The delightful citrusy aroma of Lemon oil engages the mind and aids concentration. While Lemon supports the emotional body, its major effects are experienced in the mental field. The crisp scent of Lemon oil improves one's ability to focus. Lemon is a wonderful aid for children struggling with school. It teaches individuals to be mentally present by focusing on one thing at a time. Lemon dispels confusion and bestows clarity. It counterbalances mental fatigue due to too much studying or reading. Lemon restores energy, mental flexibility, and the drive to complete a project.

Lemon is especially helpful in cases of learning issues. Whether an individual has a difficult time concentrating or feels incapable of learning, Lemon clears self-judgments such as "I'm dumb" or "I'm not a good student." Lemon calms fears and insecurities while restoring confidence in the self. Emotionally, Lemon inspires a natural playfulness and buoyancy in the heart. It assists in releasing feelings of despair and hopelessness by restoring feelings of joy and happiness. Lemon inspires joyful involvement in the present moment by infusing the soul with energy, confidence, and alertness.

NEGATIVE EMOTIONS: Confused, inability to focus, mentally fatigued, lack of joy and energy, learning issues, guilty, disengaged

POSITIVE PROPERTIES: Focused, energized, mental clarity, alert, rational, joyful

COMPANION OILS: Rosemary, Dill, Peppermint, Sunshine Blend, Focus Blend

SUGGESTED USES:
Aromatic: Inhale from bottle or diffuse before mental exertion or during work or study.

Topical: Dilute 1-3 drops with carrier oil and apply on wrists and temples.

LEMONGRASS
THE OIL OF CLEANSING

Lemongrass is a powerful cleanser of energy. It dispels feelings of despondency, despair, and lethargy. Lemongrass assists individuals in entering a healing mode or cleansing state. In this state, one easily lets go of old, limiting beliefs, toxic energies, and negativity. Lemongrass teaches individuals to move forward without hesitation. It asks them to commit to a healing path where change is a regular occurrence.

Lemongrass can also be a powerful tool in cleansing the energy within a house, room, or office space. It encourages individuals with hoarding tendencies to courageously let go of everything they no longer need.

Lemongrass also clears negative energy from the brow chakra or spiritual eyes. As individuals lets go of past issues and stagnant energy, they have an increased ability to see situations with greater clarity. It supports individuals' energy in flowing freely and smoothly. Lemongrass has a powerful mission to assist in cleansing physically, emotionally, and spiritually.

NEGATIVE EMOTIONS: Toxic or negative energy, despairing, holding on to the past, hoarding, darkness, spiritual blindness

POSITIVE PROPERTIES: Spiritual clarity, cleansing, nonattachment, simplicity, discerning, releasing what is no longer needed

COMPANION OILS: Clary Sage, Sandalwood, Oregano, Thyme, Cleansing Blend

SUGGESTED USES:
Aromatic: Inhale from bottle or diffuse.

Topical: Dilute 1-2 drops with carrier oil and apply on bottom of feet.

Environment: Add several drops into spray bottle and mist around home.

LIME

THE OIL OF ZEST FOR LIFE

Lime imbues the soul with a zest for life. When individuals have been weighed down by discouragement or grief, Lime elevates them above the mire. It instills courage and cheer in the heart and reminds them to be grateful for the gift of life.

Lime cleanses the heart, especially when there has been an accumulation of emotional toxins due to avoidance or repression. This oil revitalizes the heart space, giving room for light and joy. It clears discouragement and thoughts and feelings related to a loss of will to live. Lime shines light on the inner motives hidden in the heart and encourages emotional honesty.

Lime can also assist individuals who have overly developed their intellectual capacities but have neglected to develop themselves emotionally. This oil encourages balance between the heart and mind. It clears congestion from the heart region, assisting one in feeling safe and at home in their heart. Lime dispels apathy and resignation, and instills hope, joy, courage, and the determination to face all of life's challenges.

NEGATIVE EMOTIONS: Apathetic, resigned, grieving, loss of will to live, discouraged

POSITIVE PROPERTIES: Courageous, emotionally honest, engaged, revitalized, determined, grateful for life

COMPANION OILS: Tangerine, Melissa, Spikenard, Sunshine Blend, Joyful Blend

SUGGESTED USES:
Aromatic: Inhale from bottle or diffuse.

Topical: Dilute 1-3 drops with carrier oil and apply over chest.

LITSEA
THE OIL OF MANIFESTATION

Litsea is a powerful mobilizer of the will. It is especially helpful in encouraging individuals to follow through on their inspiration and promptings. Generally, individuals have many intuitive moments when their mind is open and connected to their higher consciousness. In this receptive state, information and energy flow freely. However, these inspirations are often shut down or discarded as individuals judge, criticize, and stifle the light they receive. Litsea invites individuals to have the confidence to act on the information given and to trust in wisdom that may be beyond current understanding.

Litsea instills courage to face the fear that comes immediately after inspiration. It reminds individuals that it takes a leap of faith into the unknown in order to manifest what has been previously unrealized. This oil also teaches that one must learn to trust the inner voice and rise above fear of rejection, being misunderstood, or the need for external confirmation.

Litsea invites individuals to recognize what clouds and distracts their internal clarity and to make the required changes to live in greater alignment. It acts as a catalyst for living in accordance with one's higher purpose and internal compass and helps individuals to get out of their own way. In this way, Litsea assists in the manifestation of infinite possibilities.

NEGATIVE EMOTIONS: Self-doubt and criticism, stifled, fear of rejection, relying on external confirmation, distracted, blocked, limited

POSITIVE PROPERTIES: Inspired, intuitive, aligned, receptive, manifesting, trust of inner voice, clarity, open to possibilities

COMPANION OILS: Blue Tansy, Clary Sage, Melissa, Lemongrass

SUGGESTED USES:
Aromatic: Inhale from bottle or diffuse.

Topical: Dilute 1-3 drops with carrier oil and apply on forehead, temples, or nape of neck.

MANUKA
THE OIL OF BEING UPHELD

Manuka is a powerful plant given as a gift to the earth to heal and bless humanity. It carries a unique energy signature that raises the vibration of those who are blessed to come into contact with it. The purposes of Manuka are multifaceted, each part adding its mission to its divine whole. Manuka's primary message is to remind individuals that they are known by the Divine. Like every flower and sparrow, each person is known, loved, and cared for. Manuka invites the heart to open to the gifts and blessings bestowed daily in abundance and to live in states of gratitude and wonder.

Manuka also offers powerful healing energy to bind up wounds, soothe troubled hearts, and nurture souls back into a state of centeredness. The gift of Manuka is in its role in transmuting suffering into transcendence. Its special alchemy transforms lower states of consciousness into higher vibrations and awareness. It facilitates a connection between heaven and earth and encourages access to that sacred space where individuals can rest and simply be upheld by the Divine.

Manuka offers energetic safety and shielding from the intense problems all around that individuals feel powerless to change. Once individuals surrender the weights and burdens they carry, they are free to connect to the overflowing divine goodness waiting for them. Manuka encourages tapping into an infinite universe of creativity and love. It invites all to access higher realms of learning, growing, serving, loving, and existing. Manuka helps individuals understand they occupy a unique space in the universe, there is always enough for them, and they will be taken care of. It reminds that even though there are things to grieve, divine love will return beauty for ashes.

NEGATIVE EMOTIONS: Wounded, abandoned, forsaken, suffering, disconnected, unsafe, powerless, burdened, grieving

POSITIVE PROPERTIES: Soothed, comforted, healing, loved, cared for, upheld, known by the Divine, grateful, transcendence, safe and shielded

COMPANION OILS: Rose, Melissa, Frankincense, Spikenard, Arborvitae, Myrrh, Copaiba, Respiratory Blend

SUGGESTED USES:
Aromatic: Inhale from bottle, diffuse, or place drops in hand, rub, and inhale.

Topical: Apply 1-3 drops over heart, on crown of head, forehead, or base of spine.

Environment: Add several drops into spray bottle and mist around body or home.

MARJORAM
THE OIL OF CONNECTION

Marjoram aids those who are unable to trust others or form meaningful relationships. This inability to trust often stems from harsh life experiences. These individuals develop a fear of close connection in relationships. They may tend toward reclusive behaviors, protecting themselves even further by abstaining from social interactions. They may also protect themselves by unconsciously sabotaging long-term relationships.

Marjoram shows the barriers they have formed to protect themselves from others. It reveals patterns of aloofness, distancing oneself from other people, or being cold. Those in need of Marjoram oil most likely use these protective coping strategies unintentionally. Deep down, they desire the intimate connection they subconsciously sabotage.

Marjoram teaches that trust is the basis for all relationships. It assists an individual in increasing their warmth and trust in social situations. Marjoram softens the heart and heals past wounds. It kindles the fires of trust in relationships so that one may fully blossom. When an individual feels safe and loved, they express their authenticity more freely. Marjoram restores trust and openness so that true bonds of love may be formed in friendships and relationships.

NEGATIVE EMOTIONS: Distrusting, emotionally aloof or distant, overly protective, emotionally isolated, reclusive, fear of rejection, self-sabotage

POSITIVE PROPERTIES: Emotionally open and connected, close relationships, softhearted, loving, ability to trust

COMPANION OILS: Cedarwood, Neroli, Geranium

SUGGESTED USES:
Aromatic: Inhale from bottle, diffuse, or place drops in hand, rub, and inhale.

Topical: Apply 1-3 drops over heart and chest.

MELALEUCA
(TEA TREE)

THE OIL OF ENERGETIC BOUNDARIES

Disinfectant by nature, Melaleuca, also known as tea tree oil, clears negative energetic baggage. It specifically releases codependent and parasitic relationships. These toxic relationships may be with people, microorganisms in the physical body, or spiritual beings. Individuals may feel drained of life force and energy, but they may not be consciously aware of the source of this energy leakage. Melaleuca helps break the negative ties in these kinds of relationships so that new, healthy connections may be formed that honor one's personal space and boundaries. This energetic "vampirism" between organisms violates the laws of nature. Melaleuca encourages an individual to connect to people and beings in ways that honor and respect others' agency. It helps individuals recognize the parts of themselves that invited and allowed these kinds of relationships to exist in the first place.

Through these empowering processes, Melaleuca encourages individuals to relinquish all forms of self-betrayal, including allowing others to take advantage of one's time, energy, or talents; letting others feed on one's energy; not standing up for oneself; or feeling responsible for the problems of others. Melaleuca assists individuals in purification practices and in releasing toxic debris.

NEGATIVE EMOTIONS: Parasitic and codependent relationships, poor boundaries, weak-willed, drained, emotional toxicity

POSITIVE PROPERTIES: Energetic boundaries, healthy and respectful connections, empowered, resilient, safe

COMPANION OILS: Clove, Outdoor Blend, Protective Blend, Lemongrass

SUGGESTED USES:
Aromatic: Inhale from bottle, diffuse, or place drops in hand, rub, and inhale.

Topical: Apply 1-3 drops on bottom of feet.

Environment: Add several drops into spray bottle and mist around home.

MELISSA
THE OIL OF LIGHT

Melissa oil awakens the soul to truth and light. It reminds individuals of who they truly are and why they came to this earth. Melissa invites one to release everything and anything that holds them back from reaching their fullest potential.

Melissa assists individuals in receiving spiritual guidance by reconnecting them with their inner voice. It uplifts the soul by preparing one to ascend. When one feels too weighed down by the burdens of life, Melissa encourages them to keep going. It gives strength and vitality to the innermost recesses of the heart and soul. This oil invites one to participate in higher realms of living and dreaming. As they stay connected to spiritual sources, they feel lightness in their being and brightness in their core. Melissa reminds everyone that each individual has a spark of divinity within them, and with love and attention, the spark will grow. This oil fuels that spark of energy, igniting an individual's True Self. Melissa assists them in shedding everything that is not in harmony with their inner light.

Melissa's enthusiasm is contagious. Through the intense light and vibration this oil has to offer, individuals may feel they cannot help but let go of feelings of darkness, despair, and other low vibrations that are holding them down. It teaches the joy of living.

NEGATIVE EMOTIONS: Despairing, hopeless, darkness, burdened, loss of will to live, overwhelmed

POSITIVE PROPERTIES: Enlightened, joyful, energized, integrity, spiritually connected, contagious enthusiasm, liberated, optimistic

COMPANION OILS: Frankincense, Copaiba, Peppermint, Tangerine, Lime

SUGGESTED USES:
Aromatic: Inhale from bottle, diffuse, or place drops in hand, rub, and inhale.

Topical: Apply 1 drop on forehead.

MYRRH
THE OIL OF MOTHER EARTH

Myrrh oil nurtures the soul's relationship with its maternal mother and with the earth. This oil supports individuals who have had disturbances with the mother-child bond. Whether it's a division between the child and the biological mother or Mother Earth herself, Myrrh can help bridge the gap and heal the disturbance. This division or lack of attachment may be related to adoption, birth trauma, malnourishment, experiences of abandonment, or other childhood issues. Myrrh helps the soul to feel the love and nurturing presence of a mother. Similar to the nutrient-rich colostrum found in a mother's milk, Myrrh oil inoculates individuals from the emotionally adverse and harmful effects of the world. Like the warmth of a mother's love for her child, Myrrh assists individuals in feeling safe and secure.

When the mother-child bond has been disrupted, the soul may lose its childlike ability to trust. Feelings of trust are replaced with feelings of fear and a belief that the world is unsafe. Myrrh assists individuals in letting go of fear. Through reestablishing a healthy connection to the earth and to one's own mother, Myrrh rekindles trust within the soul. As the individual learns to once again live in trust, confidence in the goodness of life returns and the soul feels safe and more at home.

NEGATIVE EMOTIONS: Disrupted maternal connection, distrusting, neglected, unsafe in the world, malnourished

POSITIVE PROPERTIES: safe in the world, healthy attachments, trusting, bonding, maternal connection, nurtured, loved, secure, grounded

COMPANION OILS: Rose, Frankincense, Manuka, Monthly Blend

SUGGESTED USES:
Aromatic: Inhale from bottle, diffuse, or place drops in hand, rub, and inhale.

Topical: Apply 1-3 drops over heart, chest, around navel, or on bottom of feet.

NEROLI

THE OIL OF SHARED PURPOSE & PARTNERSHIP

Neroli is a unifying and stabilizing oil. It is particularly helpful for calming troubled hearts in relationship conflict. Its influence promotes harmony in the changing dynamics of long-term relationships. Ongoing partnerships require acceptance and growth. Over time, perceived weaknesses in others come into full view, and, as a result, individuals can grow bitter, frustrated, unsympathetic, and create emotional distance from people they once loved and cherished. If left unchecked, these feelings can grow into dysfunctional and destructive thoughts and behaviors. Perceived stagnation in a relationship can cause despair and apathy, and feed a desire to blame, punish, or escape. Alternatively, Neroli invites individuals to develop the character traits of fidelity, empathy, patience, forgiveness, and resilience to ease these relationship challenges.

Neroli assists with the positive evolution of sexual intimacy between individuals who have been together long enough to experience significant contrasts in their sexual relationship. It symbolizes the fleeting beauty of spring blossoms and honors the long-lasting creation cycle in the life of the tree. Neroli aids in realizing deeper states of connection in intimate moments. It also encourages individuals to address the emotional barriers that impede healthy sexual expression and connection. Neroli gently reminds that sexual unity is a key aspect of relationship happiness, and to take the time to nurture this process.

Neroli teaches that unity blossoms from adaptation, cooperation, tolerance, perseverance, and kindness. It encourages active acceptance and supportive space for the chosen partner. Neroli invites individuals to attune their focus to the beautiful tapestry that is created as two lives intertwine to share purpose and find meaning.

NEGATIVE EMOTIONS: Conflicted, restless, impatient, bitter, frustrated, unsympathetic, disloyal, dispassionate, sexual inhibition, aloof, unkind, stagnant, blaming, escapism

POSITIVE PROPERTIES: Patient, empathetic, kind, tolerant, fidelity, calm, intimate, sexual desire, resilient, cooperative, committed

COMPANION OILS: Geranium, Jasmine, Cinnamon, Women's Blend, Marjoram, Spikenard, Monthly Blend

SUGGESTED USES:
Aromatic: Inhale from bottle, diffuse, or place drops in hand, rub, and inhale.

Topical: Apply 1-3 drops over heart, sacral chakra (lower stomach), throat, or behind ears.

OREGANO
THE OIL OF HUMILITY & NONATTACHMENT

Oregano cuts through the fluff of life and teaches individuals to do the same. It removes blocks, clears negativity, and cuts away negative attachments. Oregano is a powerful oil and may even be described as forceful or intense.

Oregano addresses a person's need to be right. Individuals in need of Oregano may attempt to convert other people to their own fixed opinions. Their strong will can make them unteachable and unwilling to budge. They hold rigidly to their opinions and belief systems. However, Oregano is resolute and has the power to break through a strong will and teach humility.

On the deepest level, Oregano dispels materialism and attachment that hinders growth and progress. While using Oregano, a person may feel encouraged to end a toxic relationship, quit an oppressive job, or end a destructive habit. These toxic attachments limit one's capacity to feel a healthy connection to the Divine. Oregano encourages true spirituality by inviting the soul to live in nonattachment and teaches that devotion to a Higher Power includes letting go of rigidity, willfulness, negative attachments, and materialism.

NEGATIVE EMOTIONS: Negative attachments, prideful, opinionated, stubborn, materialistic

POSITIVE PROPERTIES: Humble, nonattachment, willing, teachable, flexible

COMPANION OILS: Sandalwood, Thyme, Melaleuca, Lemongrass, Cypress

SUGGESTED USES:
Aromatic: Inhale from bottle or diffuse.

Topical: Dilute 1 drop or less with carrier oil and apply on bottom of feet.

> **NOTE:** Oregano can be irritating to skin; be cautious when applying topically.

PATCHOULI
THE OIL OF PHYSICALITY

Patchouli supports individuals in becoming fully present in their physical body. It balances those who feel devitalized and who seek to escape the body through spiritual pursuits or other forms of distraction. Patchouli tempers obsessive personalities by bringing them down to reality and teaching them moderation. This oil is grounding and stabilizing.

Patchouli compliments yoga practice, tai chi, or other exercises that aim to connect the spirit with the body. While using Patchouli, individuals feel more grounded and fluid. This oil calms fear and nervous tension, stilling the heart and mind in preparing the spirit and body for deeper union. It also helps individuals to stay in touch with the earth.

Patchouli helps individuals appreciate the magnificence of the physical body and all of its natural processes and functions. It assists in releasing emotional judgments and issues related to the body, such as believing the body is unholy or dirty. This oil helps with body image distortions and general body dislike. Patchouli brings confidence in the body, as well as grace, poise, and physical strength. It reminds individuals of their childhood experiences when they used their bodies for play and fun. On the deepest level, Patchouli assists an individual to feel at peace while being present in their physical body.

NEGATIVE EMOTIONS: Body shame and judgment, disconnected from body, ungrounded, body tension

POSITIVE PROPERTIES: Grounded, confident, moderation, body connection and acceptance, balanced, stable, physically expressive

COMPANION OILS: Grapefruit, Cinnamon

SUGGESTED USES:

Aromatic: Inhale from bottle, diffuse, or place drops in hand, rub, and inhale.

Topical: Apply 1-3 drops on bottom of feet or base of spine.

PEPPERMINT

THE OIL OF A BUOYANT HEART

Peppermint brings joy and buoyancy to the heart and soul. It invigorates body, mind, and spirit, and reminds individuals that life can be happy, and they don't have to be controlled by fear. It lifts an individual out of their emotional trials for a short reprieve. When individuals use Peppermint, they feel as though they're gliding through life. It assists in staying on the surface of emotional issues like floating on top of water.

The power of Peppermint can be felt most in times of discouragement or despair. When individuals are disheartened, they may use Peppermint to rediscover the joy of being alive.

However, a person may also abuse the properties of Peppermint oil. If it is used as a permanent escape to avoid dealing with emotional pain, it can hinder growth and progress. Peppermint should not be used in this way. It aids individuals who need a short breather. At times, a reprieve is necessary before reentering emotional waters, but one is not meant to wade in the shallow end forever. When it is accepted and embraced, emotional pain serves as a teacher. Peppermint can assist individuals in regaining the strength needed to face their emotional reality.

NEGATIVE EMOTIONS: Unbearable pain, intense despair, heavyhearted, pessimistic

POSITIVE PROPERTIES: Buoyant, optimistic, relieved, strength to face emotional pain

COMPANION OILS: Tangerine, Joyful Blend, Lime, Red Mandarin, Sunshine Blend

SUGGESTED USES:
Aromatic: Inhale from bottle, diffuse, or place 1 drop in hand, rub, and inhale.

Topical: Dilute 1-2 drops with carrier oil and apply over chest, on shoulders, or neck.

PETITGRAIN

THE OIL OF ANCESTRY

Petitgrain invokes a deep appreciation for positive forms of ancestral knowledge, wisdom, and family history. All individuals carry a portion of their ancestors' lives and stories within them—physically, emotionally, and through inherited traditions. Petitgrain illuminates the eternal connection to all previous generations that weaves its way through the present generation and on to the next. It reminds individuals that it was by their ancestors' sacrifice they have the opportunity to experience this life. Petitgrain invites individuals to choose to honor the good that was inherited from their family and also make the path lighter for those who follow.

In this way, Petitgrain is also a great aid in healing a complicated family history. It invites individuals to accept the humanness of their ancestors and seek to learn from their mistakes. Instead of avoiding the pain of the past, Petitgrain encourages thoughtful awareness of how to heal wounds in the family line. It reveals patterns and tendencies of unconsciously repeating family mistakes. Individuals in need of Petitgrain may be unable or unwilling to depart from their family's way of thinking. Instead, they follow in the footsteps of their predecessors and ancestral traditions. Or they feel too bound to a family story they wish to disown and desire to disconnect from the reality of the previous generations. For either extreme, Petitgrain invites healthy awareness and balance. It encourages those who view any departure from tradition as a betrayal of the family to release the fear of disapproval and forge the path that is right for them. It also reminds those who desire to disconnect from their family origins to be willing to see the positives of healthy family connection. Petitgrain invites all to see the gift of their ancestral traditions and will assist them in their efforts to heal unfinished and unresolved ancestral issues.

Petitgrain reminds individuals that through accepting their ancestry, they can find peace, clarity, wisdom, and empathy for their own journey through this life.

NEGATIVE EMOTIONS: Disowning ancestry, repeating negative family patterns, duty-bound, loyalty to unhealthy traditions, dishonoring progenitors

POSITIVE PROPERTIES: Pioneering, chain-breaking, cultivating healthy traditions, embracing positive family connections

COMPANION OILS: White Fir, Birch, Douglas Fir, Bergamot

SUGGESTED USES:
Aromatic: Inhale from bottle or diffuse.

Topical: Dilute 1-3 drops with carrier oil and apply on bottom of feet or base of spine.

RED MANDARIN
THE OIL OF CHILDLIKE PERSPECTIVE

Mandarin is one of the parent fruits of all modern citrus varieties, and is considered to be one of the sweetest of all citrus fruits. As such, Red Mandarin oil offers a unique perspective: it invites individuals to see life through childlike eyes, appreciating the sweetness, wonder, and innocence in life. Children are not as easily set back or weighed down by the cares of life. They are quicker to move on and bounce back after encountering challenges. Red Mandarin invites adults to embrace this healthier, more resilient way of existing.

Red Mandarin can also be instrumental in supporting parenting. Oftentimes parents forget the magic and miracle of the lives they have created or accepted. The demands of day-to-day living, including the stress of providing for needs, addressing emotional upheavals, and sheer physical exhaustion can dim the joy, excitement, and purpose children can offer. Parents often find themselves feeling overwhelmed, unappreciated, and unable to meet the ever-present demands. This can lead to being discouraged, frustrated, angry, and filled with self-doubt. Red Mandarin reassures that while parenting can be extremely challenging, it can also be rewarding and refining.

This oil encourages all, parents and nonparents alike, to remember the innocence of childhood. It invites them to accept that the years of influence are short; life's seasons change, and children are constantly evolving, learning, and growing. Red Mandarin refreshes the weary and careworn parent and assists them to refocus on the beauty contained in the simple moments of life with a child. However, Red Mandarin reassures all who are overwhelmed that even though adult cares and concerns can be hard, life is still full of sweet moments that deserve to be noticed.

NEGATIVE EMOTIONS: Overwhelmed, weighed down, joyless parenthood, stressed, exhausted, discouraged, burdened, jaded

POSITIVE PROPERTIES: Seeing sweetness in life, wonder in parenting, refreshed, joy in simple moments, cherishing childhood, innocent, positive perspective

COMPANION OILS: Myrrh, Frankincense, Restful Blend, Neroli, Ylang Ylang

SUGGESTED USES:
Aromatic: Inhale from bottle or diffuse.

Topical: Dilute 1-3 drops with carrier oil and apply around navel, on wrists, or behind ears.

ROMAN CHAMOMILE

THE OIL OF SPIRITUAL PURPOSE

Roman Chamomile supports individuals in discovering and living their true life's purpose. Regardless of what someone does for a living, they can find purpose and meaning in life. Purpose isn't defined simply by outward actions of individuals; it is housed within their heart and soul and radiates out to the world. As individuals live from the center of their beings, they find power and purpose that is indescribable. They also feel calmer and more at peace.

Roman Chamomile assists a person in shedding the meaningless activities that consume their lives, so they can focus on a more fulfilling work, even the work of their own souls. This oil assists in feeling connected to and supported by divine helpers and guides, and calms insecurities about following one's spiritual path. When in doubt, Roman Chamomile softens the personality, easing the overactive ego-mind. It restores one's confidence in doing what they came to this earth to do. People fearfully believe that if they do what they love, they will end up destitute. Roman Chamomile reminds them to do what they love to experience true success.

NEGATIVE EMOTIONS: Purposeless, discouraged, drudgery, frustrated, unsettled

POSITIVE PROPERTIES: Purposeful, guided, peaceful, fulfilled, relaxed, spiritually connected

COMPANION OILS: Blue Tansy, Frankincense, Anti-Aging Blend

SUGGESTED USES:
Aromatic: Inhale from bottle, diffuse, or place drops in hand, rub, and inhale.

Topical: Apply 1-2 drops on forehead or behind ears.

ROSE
THE OIL OF DIVINE LOVE

Rose oil holds a higher vibration than any other oil on the planet. It is a powerful healer of the heart. It supports individuals in reaching heavenward and connecting with divine love. Rose teaches the essential need for divine grace and intervention in the healing process. As an individual opens to receive divine benevolence in all its manifestations, the heart is softened. If one can simply let go and choose to receive divine love, they are wrapped in warmth, charity, and compassion.

Rose invites individuals to experience the unwavering, unchanging, unconditional love of the Divine. This love heals all hearts and dresses all wounds. It restores individuals to authenticity, wholeness, and purity. As one feels unconditional love and acceptance, the heart is softened. As the heart fully opens, a fountain of love flows freely through the soul. In this state, one feels charity and compassion. Charity is experienced on behalf of oneself and others. Rose embodies divine love and teaches individuals how to contact this love through prayer, meditation, and opening the heart to receive.

NEGATIVE EMOTIONS: Bereft of divine love, constricted feelings, closed or broken heart, lack of compassion, wounded

POSITIVE PROPERTIES: Loved, compassionate, healing, tenderhearted, accepted, empathy, receiving divine love

COMPANION OILS: Geranium, Anti-Aging Blend, Manuka, Arborvitae, Comforting Blend

SUGGESTED USES:
Aromatic: Inhale from bottle.

Topical: Dilute 1 drop with carrier oil and apply over heart.

ROSEMARY
THE OIL OF KNOWLEDGE & TRANSITION

Rosemary assists in the development of true knowledge and true intellect. It teaches that one can be instructed from a far greater space of understanding than the human mind. It challenges individuals to look deeper than they normally would and ask more soul-searching questions so that they may receive more inspired answers.

Rosemary assists individuals who struggle with learning disabilities. It brings expansion to the mind, supporting individuals in receiving new information and new experiences.

Rosemary aids in times of transition and change. When a person is having a difficult time adjusting to a new house, school, or relationship, this oil can assist. Rosemary teaches that one does not understand all things because they have a mortal perspective.

It invites individuals to trust in a higher, more intelligent power than themselves. It supports them in feeling confident and assured during times of great change in understanding or perspective. Rosemary roots them in the true knowledge that surpasses all understanding.

NEGATIVE EMOTIONS: Confused, difficulty adjusting or transitioning, limited perspective, difficulties with learning

POSITIVE PROPERTIES: Mental clarity, knowledgable, teachable, enlightened, open to new experiences, ability to adjust

COMPANION OILS: Dill, Lemon, Detoxification Blend

SUGGESTED USES:
Aromatic: Inhale from bottle, diffuse, or place drops in hand, rub, and inhale.

Topical: Apply 1-3 drops on nape of neck, forehead, or behind ears.

SANDALWOOD
THE OIL OF SACRED DEVOTION

Sandalwood assists with all kinds of prayer, meditation, and spiritual worship. It teaches reverence and respect for Deity. This oil has been used since ancient times for its powerful ability to calm the mind, still the heart, and prepare the spirit to commune with God.

Sandalwood teaches of spiritual devotion and spiritual sacrifice. It invites individuals to place all material attachments on the altar of sacrifice so that they may truly progress spiritually. This oil asks individuals to assess where their hearts are and challenges them to reorder their priorities to be in alignment with the Divine will.

Sandalwood assists in quieting the mind so that individuals may hear the subtle voice of the Spirit. It raises them into higher levels of consciousness. Sandalwood assists one in reaching beyond their current confines and belief systems. For those who are ready to leave behind attachment to fame, wealth, and the need for acceptance, Sandalwood teaches true humility, devotion, and love for the Divine.

NEGATIVE EMOTIONS: Disconnected from God or spiritual self, emptiness, overthinking, materialistic

POSITIVE PROPERTIES: Humble, spiritual devotion, spiritual clarity, still, surrender, connected to higher consciousness

COMPANION OILS: Oregano, Spikenard, Anti-Aging Blend, Reassuring Blend

SUGGESTED USES:
Aromatic: Inhale from bottle, diffuse, or place drops in hand, rub, and inhale before studying, meditating, or prayer.

Topical: Apply 1 drop on crown of head or forehead.

NOTE: While there are several species of Sandalwood, most of them have a very high vibration that is in harmony with the spiritual properties described here. Both Hawaiian and Indian Sandalwood oil expand the sixth chakra, or brow chakra, but Hawaiian is slightly more supportive to additional upper chakra centers while Indian promotes slightly deeper and more ancient grounding in the lower chakras. They are both excellent oils for meditation and spiritual practices.

SIBERIAN FIR

THE OIL OF AGING & PERSPECTIVE

Siberian Fir addresses generational healing from the perspective of the mature. It assists during the twilight years as individuals transition into a more full, mature awareness. This period in one's life cycle can be beset with losses of many kinds. Siberian Fir offers comfort and support during periods of grief, regret, and longing. It aids in the necessary healing and reconciliation process of a life full of mixed experiences.

Siberian Fir encourages an honest and gentle approach to assessing one's life choices, influence, and legacy. Upon reflection, all people will find moments of regret and moments they cherish. Siberian Fir teaches that without the winds of opposition, individuals would never have gained the wisdom and strength they now possess. It also reminds that forgiveness—both needing to forgive and needing to be forgiven—is integral to development.

Siberian Fir helps ease difficult transitions by encouraging individuals to focus on finding meaning and purpose with each new chapter. As they progress through life, individuals may need to realign their hopes and aspirations to the realities of the present moment. Siberian Fir offers its steady energy through periods of change and adjustment, reminding individuals to look for the good and remember that they are inherently valuable and needed. The best gift that can be given to the next generation is sharing a heart at peace.

NEGATIVE EMOTIONS: Grieving, loss, despairing, sad, regretful, fretting over the past, pining

POSITIVE PROPERTIES: Comforted, forgiveness, perspective, honest, wisdom, living in the present, optimistic, adaptable, peaceful

COMPANION OILS: White Fir, Petitgrain, Renewing Blend, Reassuring Blend, Rosemary, Comforting Blend, Encouraging Blend

SUGGESTED USES:

Aromatic: Inhale from bottle, diffuse, or place drops in hand, rub, and inhale.

Topical: Apply 1-3 drops over heart, on wrists, or bottom of feet.

SPEARMINT

THE OIL OF CONFIDENT SPEECH

Spearmint inspires clarity of thought and confident verbal expression. Individuals in need of Spearmint may hide their thoughts, opinions, and ideas by withholding their voices. Spearmint encourages inner clarity about one's personal convictions and opinions. It then assists individuals in translating that inner clarity into words.

Spearmint promotes confidence in expressing oneself verbally, especially when speaking in front of groups of people. It helps individuals create an effective stage presence by infusing them with confidence. Spearmint also encourages individuals to take a public stand on behalf of their values and opinions.

Spearmint can be a helpful remedy for those who struggle with communicating clearly for a wide range of reasons, from feeling scattered and inarticulate to stumbling over one's words. It assists individuals in becoming emotionally clear about what they want to say and then saying it. In short, Spearmint can help individuals access their inner light and convey that light to the world with clarity and confidence.

NEGATIVE EMOTIONS: Fear of public speaking, timid, holding back opinions, inarticulate

POSITIVE PROPERTIES: Confident, articulate communication, clarity, courageous

COMPANION OILS: Cassia, Lavender, Clary Sage

SUGGESTED USES:
Aromatic: Inhale from bottle or diffuse.

Topical: Dilute 1-3 drops with carrier oil and apply over throat.

SPIKENARD
THE OIL OF GRATITUDE

Spikenard encourages true appreciation for life. It addresses patterns of ingratitude, where individuals see themselves as targets of bad luck or victims of their life circumstances. This perception can often lead to feelings of blame and anger.

Spikenard encourages the soul to surrender and accept life exactly as it is. It invites individuals to let go and find an appreciation for all of life's experiences.

By opening the soul to acceptance and gratitude, Spikenard assists individuals in seeing the deeper meaning in their lives. It supports them in feeling joy and happiness for other people as well as for themselves. It invites individuals to expand by fully letting go of resistance, anger, and blame. Gratitude is an expression of complete acceptance and abundance. A grateful person is content with what they have. Spikenard teaches individuals to be grateful for their challenges as well as their blessings. It also assists individuals in transcending their sorrows through being grateful for their present life circumstances. Through complete surrender and acceptance, the soul may be brought into peace and harmony.

NEGATIVE EMOTIONS: Ungrateful, resisting, victim mentality, angry, greedy, selfish, expecting bad luck

POSITIVE PROPERTIES: Grateful, acceptance, content, peaceful

COMPANION OILS: Wild Orange, Anti-Aging Blend, Lime, Ginger, Clove

SUGGESTED USES:
Aromatic: Inhale from bottle, diffuse, or place drops in hand, rub, and inhale.

Topical: Apply 1-3 drops on wrists, forehead, or over solar plexus (upper stomach).

TANGERINE
THE OIL OF CHEER & CREATIVITY

Tangerine's strong qualities of cheer and joyfulness can lift the darkest of moods. It can assist those who feel cut off from the lightness of heart often manifested by children. Those who feel overburdened by responsibility would benefit from Tangerine's uplifting vibration. It encourages a person to be creative and spontaneous.

Creativity can be stifled by an excessive sense of duty or creating rigid standards for oneself. While work, duty, and responsibility all have their place, feeling overworked, overly responsible, and overburdened leads to a loss of creative energy. Tangerine invites individuals to make room for their creative side, and asks that they reinsert fun, joy, and spontaneity into their lives.

Tangerine supports individuals in accessing the abundant pool of creative energy held within the spirit. It then assists that energy in flowing through the heart and into physical manifestation. Tangerine teaches individuals to enjoy life by being more abundantly creative and to reexperience the joy and cheerfulness they knew in childhood.

NEGATIVE EMOTIONS: Overburdened by responsibilities, stifled creativity, duty-bound, overworked, heavyhearted, joyless

POSITIVE PROPERTIES: Cheerful, fun, creative, spontaneous, fulfilled, lighthearted, joyful, optimistic

COMPANION OILS: Uplifting Blend, Invigorating Blend, Ylang Ylang, Basil, Wild Orange, Lime, Sunshine Blend, Red Mandarin

SUGGESTED USES:
Aromatic: Inhale from bottle, diffuse, or place drops in hand, rub, and inhale.

Topical: Apply 1-2 drops on wrists, over heart, or sacral chakra (upper stomach).

THYME
THE OIL OF RELEASING & FORGIVING

Thyme is one of the most powerful cleansers of the emotional body and assists in addressing trapped feelings which have been buried for a long time. It reaches deep within the body and soul, searching for unresolved negativity. Thyme brings to the surface old, stagnant feelings. It is particularly helpful in treating the toxic emotions of hate, rage, anger, and resentment, which cause the heart to close.

Thyme empties the soul of negativity, leaving the heart wide open. In this state of openness, individuals begin to feel tolerance and patience for others. As the heart opens more and more, it is able to receive love and offer forgiveness. Thyme teaches that it's time to let go and move forward. As individuals forgive, they free themselves from emotional bondage. Thyme transforms hate and anger into love and forgiveness.

NEGATIVE EMOTIONS: Unforgiving, angry, rage, hate, bitter, resentful, emotional bondage

POSITIVE PROPERTIES: Forgiving, tolerant, patient, openhearted, understanding, emotional release

COMPANION OILS: Cardamom, Renewing Blend, Geranium, Cypress, Oregano

SUGGESTED USES:
Aromatic: Inhale from bottle or diffuse.

Topical: Dilute 1 drop or less with carrier oil and apply on chest, over sacral chakra (lower stomach), or on bottom of feet.

> **NOTE:** Thyme can be irritating to skin; be cautious when applying topically.

VETIVER

THE OIL OF CENTERING & DESCENT

Vetiver oil assists in becoming more rooted in life. Life can scatter one's energy and make individuals feel split between different priorities, people, and activities. Vetiver brings the individual back down to earth. It assists them in grounding to the physical world. Vetiver also assists individuals in deeply connecting with what they think and feel. In this way, Vetiver is incredibly supportive in all kinds of self-awareness work. It helps uncover the root of an emotional issue.

Vetiver challenges the need to escape pain. It centers individuals in their True Self and guides them downward to the root of their emotional issues. It helps them find relief but not through avoidance. Relief comes after they have traveled within and met the core of their emotional issue. Vetiver will not let them quit. It grounds them in the present moment and carries them through an emotional catharsis. The descent into the True Self assists individuals in discovering deeper facets of their being. Vetiver opens the doors to light and recovery through this downward journey.

NEGATIVE EMOTIONS: Apathetic, disconnected, scattered, stressed, ungrounded, avoiding, crisis

POSITIVE PROPERTIES: Centered, grounded, present, emotionally aware and connected

COMPANION OILS: Helichrysum, Juniper Berry, Grounding Blend

SUGGESTED USES:
Aromatic: Inhale from bottle, diffuse, or place drops in hand, rub, and inhale.

Topical: Apply 1-3 drops on bottom of feet or base of spine.

WHITE FIR
THE OIL OF GENERATIONAL HEALING

White Fir addresses generational issues. Patterns and traditions are passed down from family member to family member. Some of these patterns are positive while others are negative and destructive. Examples of negative patterns may include substance abuse, anger, codependency, physical or emotional abuse, eating issues, pride, and the need to be right.

White Fir assists the individual in unearthing these negative patterns from the hidden recesses of the body and soul. As they are brought to the light of consciousness, they can be dealt with and put to rest. Individuals can choose not to participate in destructive family patterns and thereby break the tradition. White Fir aids this process and increases one's chances of success. In breaking these patterns, it offers a refuge of spiritual protection and helps individuals stay true to the path of healing, even if their family members oppose them in leaving behind their traditions.

NEGATIVE EMOTIONS: Generational or hereditary burdens, codependent, destructive patterns, hiding

POSITIVE PROPERTIES: Generational healing, healthy patterns, healthy connections, forging new pathways, spiritual protection

COMPANION OILS: Petitgrain, Douglas Fir, Birch, Cellular Blend

SUGGESTED USES:
Aromatic: Inhale from bottle, diffuse, or place drops in hand, rub, and inhale.

Topical: Apply 3-5 drops over chest or on bottom of feet.

WILD ORANGE
THE OIL OF ABUNDANCE

Wild Orange addresses a wide variety of emotional issues. It inspires abundance, fosters creativity, and supports a positive mood. Wild Orange also reconnects individuals with their inner child and brings spontaneity, fun, joy, and playfulness into one's life.

At its core, Wild Orange teaches the true meaning of abundance. It encourages individuals to let go of scarcity mindsets with all of their manifestations, including fear, nervousness, inflexibility, workaholism, lack of humor, and the belief that there is not enough. Wild Orange reminds the soul of the limitless supply found in nature. Fruit trees, like the orange tree, give freely to all in need. This oil teaches individuals to give without thought of compensation. In nature, there is always enough to go around. Wild Orange encourages individuals to let go of their need to hoard, which is the epitome of scarcity.

Wild Orange also assists an individual's natural creative sense. It inspires limitless solutions for problems and issues. One never needs to fear. Wild Orange invites individuals to completely let go as a child does and to live from their True Self. At a person's core, they are abundance. Sharing, playing, relaxing, and enjoying the bounties of life—these are the gifts bestowed by Wild Orange oil.

NEGATIVE EMOTIONS: Scarcity, overly serious, rigid, dull, workaholic, lack of energy, discouraged, hoarding, envious

POSITIVE PROPERTIES: Abundant, sense of humor, playful, generous, spontaneous, creative, joyful

COMPANION OILS: Tangerine, Lemon, Ylang Ylang, Red Mandarin

SUGGESTED USES:
Aromatic: Inhale from bottle, diffuse, or place drops in hand, rub, and inhale.

Topical: Apply 1-3 drops over sacral chakra (upper stomach).

WINTERGREEN
THE OIL OF SURRENDER

Wintergreen is the oil of surrender. It can assist strong-willed individuals in letting go of the need to know and the need to be right. It takes great internal strength to surrender to a Higher Power. Wintergreen imbues the soul with this strength and teaches how to let go and be free of the negativity and pain one holds on to. The belief that life is painful and must be shouldered alone makes it so. Wintergreen invites individuals to surrender these strong opinions.

Wintergreen reminds individuals that they do not have to do life on their own. There is a constant invitation to surrender one's burdens to a Higher Power. All that is required is to release and let go. Wintergreen teaches that one can turn their hardships over to that power greater than themselves so they do not have to carry the burden of life all alone.

NEGATIVE EMOTIONS: Controlling, willful, needing to be right, burdened, excessive self-reliance

POSITIVE PROPERTIES: Surrender, relying on divine grace, nonattachment, teachable, strengthened

COMPANION OILS: Sandalwood, Oregano, Frankincense, Arborvitae

SUGGESTED USES:
Aromatic: Inhale from bottle or diffuse.

Topical: Dilute 1-2 drops with carrier oil and apply over heart.

YLANG YLANG

THE OIL OF THE INNER CHILD

Ylang Ylang is a powerful remedy for the heart. Modern-day society honors and reveres the mind over the heart. Yet the heart, with its intuitive ways of receiving information, is an essential part of the soul. Ylang Ylang reconnects individuals with the inner child and the pure, simple ways of the heart. It encourages play and restores a childlike nature and innocence. It assists in accessing intuition or "heart knowing."

Ylang Ylang is also a powerful remedy for releasing emotional trauma from the past. It is a fantastic support in age regression work and other methods of emotional healing. Ylang Ylang also assists individuals in releasing bottled-up emotions such as anger and sadness. Feelings that have been buried inside are brought to the light through Ylang Ylang's assistance. This oil allows emotional healing to flow naturally, nurturing the heart through the process. It reminds the individual that joy can be felt and experienced more fully by allowing the heart its full range of emotions.

NEGATIVE EMOTIONS: Joyless, stressed, overanalyzing, sad, disconnected from inner child

POSITIVE PROPERTIES: Playful, free, intuitive, emotionally connected, healing, joyful, innocent

COMPANION OILS: Geranium, Tangerine, Wild Orange, Rose, Red Mandarin

SUGGESTED USES:
Aromatic: Inhale from bottle, diffuse, or place drops in hand, rub, and inhale.

Topical: Apply 1-3 drops over heart.

SECTION III
OIL BLENDS

INTRODUCTION

HOW TO FIND A BLEND

Trademark names are not used in the Oil Blends section. However, most blends are listed in this book by the subtitle name that is found on the essential oil bottle. For example, if the blend you are looking for is Breathe, with the subtitle Respiratory Blend, look for similar oils to be listed under Respiratory Blend in this book.

ABOUT OIL BLENDS

Oil blends are created by combining several single oils to form an entirely new product. Blends are formulated to address specific physical or emotional themes or issues, and can assist with your healing by increasing the variety of emotional states which you can address. Oil blends are different from single oils but not necessarily superior. Still, blends may be more equipped than single oils in some ways. When formulated well, oil blends create synergies, or increased effectiveness, in supporting the specific issues they were created to address.

EMOTIONAL AROMATHERAPY BLENDS

Six blends in this section are labeled Emotional Aromatherapy Blends. These blends have been specially formulated to assist individuals in balancing their moods and working through their emotions, and each one targets a unique emotional state. Each blend utilizes the emotional properties of two aromatic plant families.

ANTI-AGING BLEND
THE OIL OF SPIRITUAL INSIGHT

Essential oils have been used since antiquity to assist meditation practices, prayer, and spiritual worship. Anti-Aging Blend combines the power of high vibrational oils with grounding oils to assist the connection between spirit and body, heaven and earth. It encourages positive states of being and supports the development of faith, hope, gratitude, kindness, love, patience, and trust.

Anti-Aging Blend is a wonderful aid for meditation as it quiets the mind, fosters inner stillness, and encourages spiritual growth. These oils are gentle yet powerful. They assist in the release of negativity, darkness, and limiting perceptions. This blend can mitigate spiritual blindness and other spiritual issues by offering profound light to individuals.

Anti-Aging Blend offers grace and comfort when one feels discouraged or distressed. This blend can assist individuals in transcending the darkness, pain, and stress of life. It offers support in raising levels of consciousness and preparing individuals for new heights of spiritual transformation.

INGREDIENTS: Frankincense, Sandalwood, Lavender, Myrrh, and other essential oils

NEGATIVE EMOTIONS: Spiritually disconnected, burdened, discouraged, spiritual blindness, dark night of the soul

POSITIVE PROPERTIES: Hopeful, spiritual transformation, faith, trust in the Divine, grace, still

SUGGESTED USES:
Aromatic: Inhale from bottle, diffuse, or place drops in hand, rub, and inhale.

Topical: Apply 1-3 drops on crown of head, forehead, wrists, over throat, or heart.

CELLULAR BLEND

THE OIL OF TRANSFORMATION

Cellular Blend works emotionally as well as physically with the cycles of life and death and personal transformation. By putting off the old, individuals become free to experience the new—this is transformation. Cellular Blend supports the body's sick or damaged cells to either transition to death, or to transform, repair, and renew. Through the help and support of this blend, individuals can assist their bodies, cells, energy, and emotions in returning to a balanced, healthy, and authentic state.

Cellular Blend is particularly supportive in releasing all types of negative family patterns which are recorded in the body itself (in the DNA). It is especially suited for those who struggle with debilitating circumstances, as it helps to relieve feelings of doubt, disbelief, despair, and burden. It teaches individuals to reclaim their life energy and to believe that change is possible. Cellular Blend supports the process of regaining health and vitality by encouraging the release of the old and the birth of the new.

INGREDIENTS: Frankincense, Wild Orange, Lemongrass, Thyme, Clove, and other essential oils

NEGATIVE EMOTIONS: Debilitated, discouraged, toxic, stuck, burdened by family patterns

POSITIVE PROPERTIES: Repairing, balanced, transforming, rebirth, vitality, healthy, open to change

SUGGESTED USES:
Aromatic: Inhale from bottle, diffuse, or place drops in hand, rub, and inhale.

Topical: Apply 1-3 drops on nape of neck or bottom of feet.

CLEANSING BLEND

THE OIL OF PURIFICATION

Cleansing Blend assists individuals in releasing toxic emotions and entering a cleansing state. It revitalizes the energy system, washing away negative influences. This blend supports individuals who feel trapped by negativity or toxicity. Cleansing Blend provides freedom from past habits and patterns. It is especially helpful in combating toxic feelings of hate, rage, enmeshment, and in severing other negative attachments.

Like Lemongrass, Cleansing Blend makes a wonderful space cleanser. It can clear negative energy from the household and the environment, as well as cleanse the air of odor and harmful microorganisms. Diffused in the air, these oils can facilitate emotional breakthroughs. In order to heal, one must receive. But in order to receive, one must first release what is blocking the new, clean energy from entering. Cleansing Blend supports individuals in constantly releasing the old so they may be open to the new.

INGREDIENTS: Lemon, Siberian Fir, Citronella, Lime, and other essential oils

NEGATIVE EMOTIONS: Trapped, negative, toxic, hate, rage, controlling

POSITIVE PROPERTIES: Unencumbered, cleansing, purifying, releasing

SUGGESTED USES:
Aromatic: Inhale from bottle, diffuse, or place drops in hand, rub, and inhale.

Topical: Apply 1-3 drops on bottom of feet.

Environment: Add several drops into spray bottle and mist around home.

COMFORTING BLEND

THE OIL OF CONSOLATION
EMOTIONAL AROMATHERAPY BLEND

This blend of trees and flowers was formulated to assist individuals who are in need of emotional comfort. It soothes emotional pain after periods of extreme stress or trauma. Comforting Blend assists individuals who are burdened by loss, grief, or tragedy. When past emotional hurts resurface, Comforting Blend can assist in releasing these emotional burdens.

When a storm is raging in one's heart or mind, or when there is no relief from fear, emotional pain, or anxious feelings, Comforting Blend can assist individuals in taking the first steps toward healing. It encourages individuals to seek divine intervention so they may experience the ever-present mantle of warmth, love, and consolation. Comforting Blend helps ease one's burdens, assists in experiencing a serene heart and mind, and guides individuals toward emotional rest.

INGREDIENTS: Frankincense, Patchouli, Ylang Ylang, Labdanum, Amyris, Sandalwood, and other essential oils

NEGATIVE EMOTIONS: Grieving, loss, traumatized, anxious, restless, unsettled, emotional pain, burdened

POSITIVE PROPERTIES: Comforted, content, restful, whole, serene, healing

SUGGESTED USES:
Aromatic: Inhale from bottle, diffuse, or place drops in hand, rub, and inhale.

Topical: Apply 1-3 drops over heart, behind ears, or on wrists.

DETOXIFICATION BLEND

THE OIL OF VITALITY AND TRANSITION

Detoxification Blend was designed to cleanse the organs and systems of the body. Emotionally, this blend assists during times of transition and change. It can assist an individual in detoxing old habits and limiting beliefs. When an individual has felt trapped by self-sabotaging behaviors, Detoxification Blend paves the way for new life experiences. It aids in letting go of behaviors that are destructive to one's health and happiness. It is especially helpful during major life changes which require adjustments in habit and lifestyle, such as altering diet, quitting smoking, or leaving a toxic relationship.

Detoxification Blend reawakens vital life energy. It also assists an individual in discovering new energy and vitality by encouraging the release of physical and emotional toxins. This blend aids in shedding apathy and any destructive habit, helping a person find new enthusiasm for life. As individuals let go of limiting beliefs, behaviors, and lifestyles, they have greater room to receive. As a result, they are able to see life from a fresh perspective and embrace new experiences.

INGREDIENTS: Tangerine, Rosemary, Geranium, and other essential oils

NEGATIVE EMOTIONS: Self-sabotage, difficulty with transitions, toxicity, limiting beliefs, apathetic

POSITIVE PROPERTIES: Ability to adjust, revitalized, purifying, open to new experiences

SUGGESTED USES:
Aromatic: Inhale from bottle, diffuse, or place drops in hand, rub, and inhale.

Topical: Apply 1-3 drops over solar plexus (upper stomach), on middle of back, or bottom of feet.

DIGESTIVE BLEND

THE OIL OF DIGESTION

Digestive Blend was formulated to support the body's digestive system. It also has a powerful emotional quality for supporting individuals who lack interest in life and the physical world. The individual may have a tendency to take on too much at once. This overload of information and stimulation may lead to an emotional form of indigestion, where the individual cannot break down life experiences into palatable forms. The soul literally becomes overfed and undernourished, as it cannot translate its experiences into a usable form. When individuals are fully overwhelmed and overstimulated, they may lose their appetite for food, life, and the physical world in general. They may become apathetic about their situation and begin neglecting their body's basic needs.

Digestive Blend combines powerful oils to support the body and the spirit in assimilating new information and events. It increases one's ability to receive new information, new relationships, and new experiences and be open to new possibilities. This blend aids individuals in digesting life's many experiences.

INGREDIENTS: Anise, Peppermint, Ginger, Caraway, Coriander, and other essential oils

NEGATIVE EMOTIONS: Overstimulated, loss of appetite for food or life, difficulty assimilating new information or experiences, overwhelmed, apathetic, unenthusiastic

POSITIVE PROPERTIES: Assimilating experiences, adjusting, nourished, enthusiastic

SUGGESTED USES:
Aromatic: Inhale from bottle, diffuse, or place drops in hand, rub, and inhale.

Topical: Apply 1-3 drops over entire stomach.

ENCOURAGING BLEND

THE OIL OF MOTIVATION
EMOTIONAL AROMATHERAPY BLEND

This blend of mints and citrus oils was formulated for those who need motivation and encouragement. It assists individuals whose will has stagnated and needs to be fired into action again. Encouraging Blend fosters confidence to follow through with one's creative inspirations and intentions. It also imbues a warrior-like spirit and strengthens individuals to face adversities and challenges.

This blend is especially helpful in times of weariness and discouragement when one has lost the energy and motivation to complete important life tasks, such as caring for a sick loved one or assisting others in need. It is easy to become lethargic or discouraged when one is in a long-term care situation or another emotionally or physically taxing circumstance. Encouraging Blend can act as a support in rediscovering and maintaining one's desire to serve. It encourages individuals to work through their feelings of gloom, weariness, or hopelessness, rather than slipping into despondency or despair. Instead of remaining paralyzed by these feelings, this blend launches individuals into positive action. It confidently reassures that they do have the courage needed to face another day.

INGREDIENTS: Peppermint, Clementine, Coriander, Basil, Yuzu, Melissa, and other essential oils

NEGATIVE EMOTIONS: Weary, discouraged, stagnant, gloomy, lacking motivation, unable to press on

POSITIVE PROPERTIES: Motivated, encouraged, hopeful, energized, confident

SUGGESTED USES:

Aromatic: Inhale from bottle or diffuse.

Topical: Dilute 1-3 drops with carrier oil and apply over solar plexus (upper stomach), heart, on wrists, or behind ears.

FOCUS BLEND

THE OIL OF PRESENCE

In contrast to Lemon oil, known as "The Oil of Focus," Focus Blend calms the mind, facilitating inner peace. Whereas Lemon activates the mind, Focus Blend quiets and grounds mental forces. It is especially beneficial to those with a short attention span. It encourages individuals to remain present with the task at hand and to complete a project, goal, or activity before moving onto the next. Focus Blend is therefore supportive to individuals who become lost in thought—those who rapidly jump from one activity or idea to the next—as well as those who lose themselves in daydreams or fantasy.

Focus Blend gently guides the soul into full awareness of its physical body and physical surroundings. It invites individuals to accept the reality of their life situation, so they may deal with it appropriately. This blend especially encourages individuals to live in the here and now, and therefore promotes a meditative state. Focus Blend's stability and grounding energy supports a healthy connection between the body and the mind. With the support of Focus Blend, individuals are empowered to live fully connected in the present moment.

INGREDIENTS: Amyris, Patchouli, Frankincense, Lime, Ylang Ylang, and other essential oils

NEGATIVE EMOTIONS: Distracted, not present or aware, daydreaming, procrastinating, scattered

POSITIVE PROPERTIES: Focused, completion of projects and tasks, living in the present moment, calm, grounded

SUGGESTED USES:
Aromatic: Inhale from bottle, diffuse, or place drops in hand, rub, and inhale.

Topical: Apply 1-3 drops on temples, wrists, or nape of neck.

GROUNDING BLEND
THE OIL OF GROUNDING

Grounding Blend is primarily a combination of tree oils and roots. Trees live in the present moment. They are not in a hurry; they are stable. Grounding Blend's soft energy is excellent for calming overactive children who have difficulty settling down. It is also a wonderful remedy for those who need to reconnect with their roots. Grounding Blend strengthens a connection with the lower body and with the earth. These connections are especially important when the upper faculties have been overused due to excessive thinking, speaking, or spiritual activity.

Grounding Blend is especially suited for personalities who seek to escape from life through disconnection or disassociation. These individuals may avoid long-term commitments in work or relationships, preferring instead to drift. This blend reminds individuals that to realize their true dreams and desires, they must stay focused on a goal until it is actualized in the physical world. Grounding Blend teaches true perseverance by assisting individuals in staying present with a specific plan or idea until it is embodied. Providing inner strength and fortitude, Grounding Blend teaches individuals to ground their energy and to manifest their vision with the patience of a tree.

INGREDIENTS: Spruce, Ho Wood, Frankincense, Blue Tansy, and other essential oils

NEGATIVE EMOTIONS: Scattered, ungrounded, disconnected, unstable

POSITIVE PROPERTIES: Grounded, stable, connected, committed, self-contained, inner strength, persevering

SUGGESTED USES:
Aromatic: Inhale from bottle, diffuse, or place drops in hand, rub, and inhale.

Topical: Apply 1-3 drops on base of spine or bottom of feet.

HOLIDAY BLEND
THE OIL OF CENTERED CELEBRATION

Holiday Blend invites people to come together and experience the warmth and comfort of positive relationships. It fosters feelings of joy, celebration, and excitement. However, personal memories and experiences of past holidays directly impact how this blend is received. Holiday Blend can simultaneously illuminate the rifts, barriers, and unhealed issues carried in families while assisting in the restoration of healthy connections by instilling a desire for togetherness and reconciliation. Coming face-to-face with these realities, compounded by the modern stresses of commercialized holidays, can trigger tension, defensiveness, hypersensitivity, and volatile emotions. This can be especially common during holiday activities with family and close communities. As such, this blend cultivates a spirit of simplification, peace, and connectedness as the focus of the holidays.

Holiday Blend can also comfort individuals who are either without family or have estranged relationships due to distance or the inability to heal. While emotionally distancing may be appropriate in some situations where extreme or abusive behaviors are present, this blend reminds that separation is most often not a long-term solution. It offers a gentle reminder to embrace the love and warmth that healthy family relationships can bring.

Additionally, Holiday Blend teaches the importance of boundaries in healthy family relationships. This is especially true for individuals who over-give. Oftentimes the desire to please others causes neglect of personal needs and wants. This blend invites individuals to evaluate their motivations of self-validation, compulsion, or guilt. While on the surface this self-sacrifice may seem altruistic, inappropriate giving leads to resentment in both the giver and receiver and is not sustainable. Holiday Blend teaches that personal energy conservation and balanced giving, combined with a nurtured sense of self, lead to the healthiest relationships and the most joyful holiday celebrations.

INGREDIENTS: Siberian Fir, Wild Orange, Clove, Cinnamon, Cassia, and other essential oils

NEGATIVE EMOTIONS: Stressed, estranged, closed, cold, hypersensitive, defensive, poor boundaries, imbalanced giving

POSITIVE PROPERTIES: Warm, emotionally safe and connected, balanced, joyful, celebratory

SUGGESTED USES:
Aromatic: Inhale from bottle or diffuse.

Environment: Add several drops into spray bottle and mist around home.

U.S. Suicide Prevention Hotline: 1-800-273-8255

National Human Trafficking Hotline: 1-888-373-7888

National Sexual Assault Hotline: 1-800-656-4673

National Domestic Violence Hotline: 1-800-799-7233

HOPE BLEND

THE OIL OF OVERCOMING

Hope was blended to bring light into the darkest places. When individuals have fallen into despair and feel there is no reason to carry on living, Hope Blend reaches out with its reassuring message that there is always a reason to hold on to hope. It encourages the belief that a brighter day will come and helps rally the internal resources needed to keep going.

Hope Blend combines the healing properties of Bergamot, Ylang Ylang, and Frankincense to address feelings of being unloved, unworthy, abandoned, and filled with shame. It helps overcome emotions associated with lost innocence, stolen childhoods, and unthinkable trauma.

Hope Blend reveals the truth: that people are not their story, their pain, or even their experiences. All individuals are beings filled with a light that can never be taken, destroyed, or diminished. This blend reassures that broken things can mend, hearts can heal, and lives can be restored. Through the darkness, its message calls out to hold on, gather strength, and have courage to believe that life matters and there is still a reason to hope.

INGREDIENTS: Bergamot, Ylang Ylang, Frankincense, and other essential oils

NEGATIVE EMOTIONS: Despairing, hopeless, unloved, traumatized, shameful

POSITIVE PROPERTIES: Hopeful, courageous, self-acceptance, believing, healing, rebirth

SUGGESTED USES:
Aromatic: Inhale from bottle, diffuse, or place drops in hand, rub, and inhale.

Topical: Apply 1-3 drops over heart, on nape of neck, or behind ears.

INSPIRING BLEND

THE OIL FOR FINDING YOUR PASSION
EMOTIONAL AROMATHERAPY BLEND

This blend was formulated to assist individuals who are lacking inner passion. It is helpful for those caught in patterns of self-denial or regimentation. Overworking and being too serious can dull one's sensitivity and emotions. When individuals are burdened by a joyless sense of duty, Inspiring Blend encourages them to be more playful and spontaneous. It teaches that there is more to living than working and obligation.

When appropriate, Inspiring Blend encourages individuals to take risks, to confidently face their fears, and to break free from the limitations they place on themselves. It challenges individuals to use their creativity and imagination to fulfill their true life's passions. In short, when life has become a dull set of routines and obligations, Inspiring Blend acts as a reminder to rediscover one's inner passion.

INGREDIENTS: Cardamom, Cinnamon, Ginger, Clove, Sandalwood, Jasmine, and other essential oils

NEGATIVE EMOTIONS: Self-denial, regimented, duty-bound, serious, dull, joyless, dispassionate

POSITIVE PROPERTIES: Passionate, risk-taking, vitality, inspired, alive, playful, spontaneous, creative

SUGGESTED USES:
Aromatic: Inhale from bottle or diffuse.

Topical: Dilute 1-3 drops with carrier oil and apply over entire stomach, on wrists, or behind ears.

INVIGORATING BLEND

THE OIL OF CREATIVITY

Invigorating Blend acts as a powerful fire starter. It returns motivation and drive when lacking. These oils are wonderful for addressing lethargy, discouragement, despondency, or a low will to live. When the soul has lost its connection to the magic in life, this blend helps restore the spark.

Invigorating Blend also inspires creativity. Every soul has a need to create. This blend inspires creative expression by reconnecting individuals with their inner child and their natural creative sense. It assists individuals in living abundantly and spontaneously, and encourages play and excitement. Invigorating Blend can motivate individuals to use their true creative power by letting go of old limitations and insecurities. It takes courage to put oneself out there artistically. Citruses bring color and imagination to one's life. This combination of oils restores confidence in oneself and in one's creations. Invigorating Blend rekindles the fire of the personality and fills the heart with creativity and joy.

INGREDIENTS: Wild Orange, Lemon, Grapefruit, Mandarin, Bergamot, Tangerine, and other essential oils

NEGATIVE EMOTIONS: Stifled creativity or artistic expression, insecure, unmotivated, disengaged, discouraged

POSITIVE PROPERTIES: Invigorated, childlike, creative, motivated, confident expression, spontaneous

SUGGESTED USES:
Aromatic: Inhale from bottle, diffuse, or place drops in hand, rub, and inhale.

Topical: Apply 1-3 drops on wrists or over solar plexus (upper stomach).

JOYFUL BLEND

THE OIL OF JOY

Joyful Blend was formulated to overcome feelings of despair and hopelessness. This blend combines powerful mood-stabilizing oils with joy-filled oils that evoke happiness. The warm vibrations of these oils can soothe the heart and balance the emotions.

Joyful Blend can assist individuals in letting go of lower energy vibrations. Negative habits lose their appeal as an individual shifts into higher levels of consciousness. This blend can raise one's energy levels and energetic vibrations into higher states. It can inspire feelings of cheerfulness, brightness, courage, relaxation, humor, playfulness, and fun. It teaches that worry and fear are not productive, but faith, hope, and determination are. These oils redirect the brain pathways to transform despair into happiness, joy, and abundance. Joyful Blend supports individuals in flowing with life while remaining in peace and light.

INGREDIENTS: Lavandin, Lavender, Sandalwood, Tangerine, Elemi, Melissa, Ylang Ylang, and other essential oils

NEGATIVE EMOTIONS: Despairing, discouraged, heavyhearted, trapped in low energy

POSITIVE PROPERTIES: Joyful, bright, optimistic, carefree, elevated, cheerful, abundant

SUGGESTED USES:
Aromatic: Inhale from bottle, diffuse, or place drops in hand, rub, and inhale.

Topical: Apply 1-3 drops on forehead, behind ears, or over heart.

MASSAGE BLEND

THE OIL OF RELAXATION

Massage Blend assists the body in calming, relaxing, and releasing physical tension. On an emotional level, Massage Blend moves an individual from stiffness of heart and mind to openness and flexibility. This blend is soothing to both body and mind, and offers comfort in times of grief and sorrow.

Most people seek out massage when they are tense or stressed. Through bodywork and massage, individuals are able to relax tight muscles. Breathing may begin to regulate, slow, and deepen. As the body relaxes, so does the mind. As muscles release tension, the heart can reopen to life. Circulation is enhanced, as is one's ability to move with life and allow things to flow. This is the gift of Massage Blend—the ability to relax, open, and move in harmony once more with the body and with existence.

INGREDIENTS: Cypress, Peppermint, Marjoram, Basil, and other essential oils

NEGATIVE EMOTIONS: Tense, stressed, rigid, unable to relax, inflexible

POSITIVE PROPERTIES: Relaxed, balanced, flexible, comforted, open mind and heart

SUGGESTED USES:
Aromatic: Inhale from bottle, diffuse, or place drops in hand, rub, and inhale.

Topical: Massage 1-3 drops wherever emotional or physical tension is experienced.

METABOLIC BLEND

THE OIL OF INNER BEAUTY

In addition to supporting the physical aspects of weight loss, this blend may also be used to address the emotional patterns which underlie and contribute to one's weight. Individuals in need of Metabolic Blend may set strict standards for themselves in diet or weight-loss programs. They believe that by denying themselves dietary pleasures and controlling their bodies, they will force their desired result. Instead, their punitive withholding is met with whiplash from the body as it desperately seeks to survive. The need for foods and sweets becomes excessive, resulting in swings in diet, weight, and mood. This usually causes discouragement and feeling out of control, as individuals berate themselves with criticism and self-hatred.

Metabolic Blend can support individuals in releasing the heavy emotions which contribute to physical and emotional pounds. It encourages them to find feelings of self-worth. As they accept their body as it is, the body can more easily move toward its ideal expression. Metabolic Blend encourages individuals to rise above self-judgment by embracing the body's natural beauty and inherent value, regardless of weight, shape, or size.

INGREDIENTS: Grapefruit, Lemon, Peppermint, and other essential oils

NEGATIVE EMOTIONS: Self-criticism, worthless, disgust or hate for physical appearance, strict, self-judgment, body shame

POSITIVE PROPERTIES: Worthy, self-acceptance, confident, embracing the body's individual beauty

SUGGESTED USES:
Aromatic: Inhale from bottle or diffuse.

Topical: Dilute 1-3 drops with carrier oil and apply anywhere body needs additional love and approval.

MONTHLY BLEND

THE OIL OF VULNERABILITY

Monthly Blend encourages warmth in relationships, stabilizes physical and emotional imbalances, and fosters emotional intimacy. It is a perfect blend for supporting pregnancy and child delivery, as it strengthens the mother-child bond. This blend assists women in accepting their maternal instincts and nurturing qualities.

Monthly Blend assists relationships by teaching individuals to be emotionally open and vulnerable. It eases the fear of rejection and encourages individuals to receive true warmth and love in their relationships. It also encourages feelings of empathy for others by reminding them to stay receptive to the thoughts, feelings, and needs of other people.

This blend works as a powerful emotional stabilizer, especially during menstruation or menopause. It releases emotional tension within the reproductive organs and helps release the expectations of suffering and dread related to the monthly cycle. In short, Monthly Blend encourages emotional intimacy and vulnerability.

INGREDIENTS: Clary Sage, Lavender, Bergamot, Roman Chamomile, Ceadarwood, Ylang Ylang, Geranium, Fennel, and other essential oils

NEGATIVE EMOTIONS: Invulnerable, guarded, emotional tension, dread of suffering during menstruation or menopause

POSITIVE PROPERTIES: Vulnerable, receptive, serene, empathetic, nurturing, bonding

SUGGESTED USES:
Aromatic: Inhale from bottle, diffuse, or place drops in hand, rub, and inhale.

Topical: Apply 1-3 drops over sacral chakra (lower stomach) or on wrists.

OUTDOOR BLEND

THE OIL OF SHIELDING

Outdoor Blend was formulated as an insect repellent, but it also offers so much more. This blend helps individuals stay calm in the face of danger or attack. Outdoor Blend strengthens the protective shield around one's body, helping them to feel safe. This is especially important for children and adults who unconsciously merge with other people's energy. They may do this as a way to relieve others' burdens, or to simply lighten the load in the environment. Regardless of the motives, this type of energetic merging weakens individuals' energy systems. Babies and young children are especially susceptible to trying to carry loved ones' feelings for them, as they struggle to know which emotions are theirs and which belong to other people. This blend can assist individuals in separating their own energy from another's.

While the confusion between boundaries is often unintentional, there are also those who would target or attack others. Outdoor Blend teaches individuals to hold strong boundaries and not allow themselves to be pushed around. It imbues individuals with courage and confidence to stand up for themselves and face their attackers.

INGREDIENTS: Ylang Ylang, Tamanu, Nootka, Cederwood, Litsea, and other essential oils

NEGATIVE EMOTIONS: Unprotected, attacked, defenseless, poor boundaries

POSITIVE PROPERTIES: Courageous, confident, self-contained, safe, strong boundaries

SUGGESTED USES:
Aromatic: Inhale from bottle, diffuse, or place drops in hand, rub, and inhale.

Topical: Place 1 drop in hand, rub, and brush over clothes.

Environment: Add several drops into spray bottle and mist on body or around home.

PROTECTIVE BLEND
THE OIL OF PROTECTION

This combination of oils is generally used to shield individuals from bacteria, mold, and viruses. This blend's protective properties, however, extend beyond the physical level by aiding individuals in warding off energetic parasites, domineering personalities, and other negative influences. Protective Blend strengthens one's immune system, which governs the ability to defend against attacks from physical pathogens and negative energies.

Protective Blend is incredibly helpful for strengthening the inner self along with inner resolve to stand up for oneself and live in integrity. This blend is especially indicated for personalities who have a weakened boundary due to some kind of perpetual violation to their personal space. Protective Blend gives individuals strength to say "no" and resolve to maintain clear boundaries. It cuts away unhealthy connections such as codependency, parasitic relationships, or emotional viruses found in negative group thought. Protective Blend greatly assists individuals in learning to stand up for themselves and live in integrity with their True Self.

INGREDIENTS: Wild Orange, Clove, Cinnamon, and other essential oils

NEGATIVE EMOTIONS: Attacked, unprotected, vulnerable, controlled, manipulated, susceptible to peer pressure

POSITIVE PROPERTIES: Healthy boundaries, protected, capable, integrity, independent, reinforced, strengthened

SUGGESTED USES:
Aromatic: Inhale from bottle or diffuse.

Topical: Dilute 1-3 drops with carrier oil and apply over chest, throat, or on bottom of feet.

Environment: Add several drops into spray bottle and mist around home.

REASSURING BLEND

THE OIL OF PEACE
EMOTIONAL AROMATHERAPY BLEND

This blend was formulated to assist individuals who lack inner peace. People thrive when they feel connected to the Divine. Souls achieve true and lasting peace through connection to this source. Without this true peace, there is a human tendency to try to manufacture peace by controlling one's environment and relationships. Especially when one feels afraid, it is tempting to try to control others because it gives an artificial sense of order and safety.

Reassuring Blend invites individuals to connect to the true source of unending peace and let go of control and excess attachments in order to experience the incredible peace that flows from the Divine. It invites individuals to trust in divine goodness and grace. Reassuring Blend affirms that no amount of control or effort can fill the empty soul. It reminds individuals that only by connecting to the Divine will they cultivate lasting peace.

INGREDIENTS: Vetiver, Lavender, Ylang Ylang, Frankincense, Clary Sage, Marjoram, and other essential oils

NEGATIVE EMOTIONS: Controlling, attached, afraid, spiritually disconnected, unsafe

POSITIVE PROPERTIES: Peaceful, serene, content, still, spiritually connected

SUGGESTED USES:
Aromatic: Inhale from bottle, diffuse, or place drops in hand, rub, and inhale.

Topical: Apply 1-3 drops over heart or throat.

RENEWING BLEND

THE OIL OF FORGIVING
EMOTIONAL AROMATHERAPY BLEND

This blend was formulated to assist individuals who desire to forgive. It is well understood that forgiving others actually sets one free. This blend is especially helpful when individuals feel cynical or begin to expect the worst from other people. Instead of looking for the good in others, they may view them in a negative light. They may also have a tendency to feel justified in blaming others for their own personal situations or misfortunes. Renewing Blend teaches that everyone is learning and growing together. Mistakes and offenses will happen but should be met with forgiveness and kindness.

Renewing Blend challenges individuals to let go of bitterness and hostilities and to embrace other people as an extension of themselves, as part of the human family. It reminds individuals to live by the Golden Rule—to treat others the way they themselves would like to be treated. It invites individuals to free themselves by realizing that others are usually doing the best they can and deserve compassion and forgiveness.

INGREDIENTS: Spruce, Bergamot, Juniper Berry, Myrrh, Arborvitae, Nootka, and other essential oils

NEGATIVE EMOTIONS: Unforgiving, critical, judgmental, resentful, cynical, bitter, blaming, angry

POSITIVE PROPERTIES: Forgiving, light, free, loving, understanding, tolerant, emphathetic

SUGGESTED USES:
Aromatic: Inhale from bottle or diffuse.

Topical: Dilute 1-3 drops with carrier oil and apply over heart, on neck, wrists, or behind ears.

RESPIRATORY BLEND

THE OIL OF BREATH

Respiratory Blend addresses the inability to let go of grief and pain. Individuals in need of Respiratory Blend struggle to breathe and literally feel suffocated by sadness. The lungs and air passages become constricted, preventing air and emotion from releasing. The root of this condition is feeling unloved; individuals grieve the love they never received. They often shut down due to fear, not knowing whether the love they need will be there. They distrust whether it's safe to open and take in life. Respiratory Blend encourages individuals to release grief and sadness and to receive genuine love and healing.

Respiratory Blend also supports one's relationship with spirit and deepens one's connection to life. It invites individuals to let go (breathe out) and receive (breathe in). In this way, this blend teaches individuals to embrace life through breath. Respiratory Blend imbues individuals with the courage to fully open.

INGREDIENTS: Laurel (Bay), Eucalyptus, Peppermint, Melaleuca, Lemon, and other essential oils

NEGATIVE EMOTIONS: Sad, grieving, despairing, unloved, constricted, distrusting, closed

POSITIVE PROPERTIES: Loved, supported, receiving, open, healing, solace, embracing life

SUGGESTED USES:
Aromatic: Inhale from bottle or diffuse.

Topical: Dilute 1-3 drops with carrier oil and apply over heart or chest.

RESTFUL BLEND

THE OIL OF TRANQUILITY

Restful Blend has a powerful effect on the mind and heart. It is a uniquely calming blend that invites individuals to relinquish feelings of stress, anxiousness, and being overwhelmed. Restful Blend can support those who struggle with an overactive mind and inability to unwind. From feelings of responsibility to feelings of worry, Restful Blend assists in quieting the mind, releasing agitation, and inviting calm.

When individuals overidentify with responsibilities or fears, they create emotional states that do not support proper rest, relaxation, and rejuvenation. Driven by constant pressures and perceived burdens, individuals struggle to keep up with the demands of their lives. This blend powerfully addresses the underlying states that are often the cause of restlessness, stress, and imbalance.

Restful Blend encourages individuals to first reconnect with themselves and discover the peace that lies within, and then to reconnect with the humanity in others. It invites individuals to acknowledge when they feel out of balance and allow time and space for true renewal. It also gently reminds that others are often caught in similar cycles of imbalance and encourages compassion and acceptance of them. Restful Blend brings a sense of tranquility that allows space for personal reflection, peace, and healing.

INGREDIENTS: Lavender, Cedarwood, Ho Wood, Ylang Ylang, Marjoram, Roman Chamomile, Vetiver, and other essential oils

NEGATIVE EMOTIONS: Stressed, emotional overload, agitated, restless, anxious, disconnected

POSITIVE PROPERTIES: Calm, tranquil, peaceful, relaxed, compassionate, connected

SUGGESTED USES:

Aromatic: Inhale from bottle, diffuse, or place drops in hand, rub, and inhale.

Topical: Apply 1-3 drops on temples, shoulders, neck, or wrists.

SOOTHING BLEND

THE OIL OF SURRENDERING PAIN

Soothing Blend is generally used for physical pain, but it can also assist individuals who are resisting or avoiding the emotions that underlie their physical pain. It offers strength to face emotional wounds, allowing the wounds to surface for transformation and healing. This blend can teach individuals how to be the observer of their painful experiences rather than overidentifying with them. When individuals suffer from intense emotional or physical pain, it is common for them to act irrationally or lose their head. Soothing Blend can support the mind in staying cool and collected, regardless of the emotional turmoil or physical pain one may be in. In this way, they maintain mental clarity in the face of danger or pain.

At its core, Soothing Blend teaches individuals acceptance and tolerance of their pain. It reveals the possibility that pain is not cruel or bad but is simply a teacher. Instead of resisting pain, one may embrace the lessons it has to offer. As individuals let go of resistance, pain lessens and often dissipates altogether. By understanding the nature of pain, this blend encourages an assimilation of all life's experiences.

INGREDIENTS: Wintergreen, Camphor, Peppermint, Ylang Ylang, Helichrysum, Blue Tansy, and other essential oils

NEGATIVE EMOTIONS: Resisting pain, avoiding emotional issues, panicked, fearful, wounded

POSITIVE PROPERTIES: Strengthened, accepting, soothed, serene, healing

SUGGESTED USES:
Aromatic: Inhale from bottle or diffuse.

Topical: Dilute 1-3 drops with carrier oil and massage wherever emotional or physical pain is experienced.

SUNSHINE BLEND

THE OIL OF ENJOYMENT

Sunshine Blend's message is all about embracing carefree moments. It insists individuals take time to reconnect and remember the childlike part of the soul that is unburdened by the stresses, worries, and seriousness of life. Most adults struggle to let go of the responsibility and demands of their lives even for a short time. This results in a fettered, heavy feeling that can only find an antidote in laughter and play.

When individuals find themselves feeling stagnant, cynical, perfectionistic, apathetic, or stifled, Sunshine Blend invites them to throw off the shackles and embrace the optimism, enthusiasm, and spontaneity of youth. It clearly reminds that creativity needs to be fed with humor, curiosity, and healthy risk. The soul craves new and exhilarating experiences to flourish and shine. This blend invites individuals to embrace the abundance all around them and to believe that they too were meant for lighthearted moments and a simpler existence. Sunshine Blend's message is simple: it's time to stop stressing and start playing!

INGREDIENTS: Grapefruit, Wild Orange, and other essential oils

NEGATIVE EMOTIONS: Stressed, burdened, overly serious and responsible, stagnant, cynical, perfectionistic, stifled

POSITIVE PROPERTIES: Childlike, carefree, playful, optimistic, enthusiastic, spontaneous, sense of humor

SUGGESTED USES:
Aromatic: Inhale from bottle, diffuse, or place drops in hand, rub, and inhale.

Topical: Apply 1-3 drops over solar plexus (upper stomach) or on wrists.

TENSION BLEND
THE OIL OF RELIEF

Generally used to relieve headaches, Tension Blend also assists individuals in releasing the stress and emotional tension that may have contributed to or caused their headache.

Tension Blend synergistically combines the powerful relaxation qualities of essential oils to assist and teach the body how to calm and relax. It can also help individuals release the fears that create tension and pain in the body. Tension Blend can calm severe stress, soothe trauma, and bring balance to the body and energy system. This blend also helps in regaining equilibrium following periods of overwork, burnout, and fatigue.

As physical and emotional discomforts are relieved, Tension Blend fosters feelings of appreciation. It invites balance and reminds individuals there is still much to be grateful for despite opposition, trials, or setbacks.

INGREDIENTS: Wintergreen, Lavender, Peppermint, Frankincense, Cilantro, Marjoram, Roman Chamomile, and other essential oils

NEGATIVE EMOTIONS: Stressed, overworked, nervous, burned out, overwhelmed, fatigued, imbalanced, tense

POSITIVE PROPERTIES: Equilibrium, calm, relaxed, relieved, grateful

SUGGESTED USES:
Aromatic: Inhale from bottle, diffuse, or place drops in hand, rub, and inhale.

Topical: Apply 1-3 drops on head, neck, and shoulders.

TOPICAL BLEND

THE OIL OF ACCEPTING IMPERFECTIONS

Topical Blend was formulated for acne and general skin health. Its major ingredient, Black Cumin seed, is not an essential oil, but has trace amounts of essential oil within it. Black Cumin is prized in many Islamic countries for its healing properties. Topical Blend combines the healing properties of Black Cumin with other essential oils.

Topical Blend emotionally supports those with suppressed anger, guilt, and self-judgment. Individuals in need of this blend may harbor feelings of guilt or anger from the past. These deeply buried feelings may exist outside their conscious awareness. Yet these feelings of pain or anger literally "boil" to the surface. If individuals do not deal with these feelings appropriately, they may manifest through lashing out or blaming others.

This blend supports individuals by increasing self-acceptance and self-love. It assists them in seeing their inherent worth, regardless of physical appearance. It encourages the healthy release and expression of feelings of anger. Topical Blend invites individuals to look past imperfections and to replace self-judgment with self-acceptance.

INGREDIENTS: Black Cumin, Rosewood, Eucalyptus, Geranium, and other essential oils

NEGATIVE EMOTIONS: Emotional pain, angry, self-judgment, concealing, supressing, blaming

POSITIVE PROPERTIES: Self-acceptance, self-love, worthy, healthy expression, self-aware

SUGGESTED USES:
Aromatic: Inhale from bottle, diffuse, or place drops in hand, rub, and inhale.

Topical: Apply anywhere body needs additional love and approval.

UPLIFTING BLEND

THE OIL OF CHEER
EMOTIONAL AROMATHERAPY BLEND

This blend of citruses and spices was formulated to assist those who are in need of cheerfulness. It is especially helpful for individuals who feel heavyhearted or who have been weighed down by many challenges in life. Encountering repeated trials over an extended period of time can have crippling effects, and may even create an expectation of permanent suffering with no hope of relief.

Uplifting Blend encourages individuals who are overcome by feelings of hopelessness and helplessness. It helps restore one's hope when they have been stretched beyond the limits of their endurance. This blend inspires faith that life will work out for the best despite difficulties and setbacks. Uplifting Blend reminds individuals there is so much more to life than the hardship they are experiencing, and to determinedly hold on until they regain the hope and joy they feel they've lost.

INGREDIENTS: Wild Orange, Clove, Star Anise, Lemon Myrtle, Nutmeg, Vanilla, and other essential oils

NEGATIVE EMOTIONS: Weighed down, hopeless, joyless, heavyhearted, depleted, helpless

POSITIVE PROPERTIES: Hopeful, comforted, believing, cheerful, uplifted, joyful, determined, restored

SUGGESTED USES:
Aromatic: Inhale from bottle or diffuse.

Topical: Dilute 1-3 drops with carrier oil and apply over heart, on forehead, or wrists.

WOMEN'S BLEND
THE OIL OF FEMININITY

The benefits of Women's Blend are not limited to women alone. While this blend possesses a strong feminine quality, female energy is often needed by both men and women.

Women's Blend softens overly masculine individuals by getting them in touch with their feminine side. It encourages letting go of pride and tough exteriors, and allows gentleness and emotional connection. It is also particularly helpful when dealing with issues that manifest as anger, hostility, or resistance toward women.

Women's Blend also assists individuals in healing their relationships with their mothers, grandmothers, and other women. It helps one reconnect with their mother when there has been strain, separation, loss, or abuse in the relationship. Both men and women can reject the feminine aspect of sexuality as a result of traumatic experiences. This blend challenges individuals to work through issues relating to femininity and sexuality. If one has rejected their feminine energy, isolated from women, or disconnected sexually, this blend invites them to heal wounds and find balance by reconnecting with positive femininity.

INGREDIENTS: Patchouli, Bergamot, Sandalwood, Rose, Vanilla, Jasmine, Cinnamon, and other essential oils.

NEGATIVE EMOTIONS: Blocked or imbalanced female energy, overly masculine, anger or resistance toward women, women issues, repressed sexuality, disconnected from mother

POSITIVE PROPERTIES: Acceptance of femininity, kind, gentle, connected to mother, healthy sexuality

SUGGESTED USES:
Aromatic: Inhale from bottle, diffuse, or place drops in hand, rub, and inhale.

Topical: Apply 1-3 over sacral chakra (lower stomach) or heart.

SECTION IV
APPENDICES

APPENDIX A
DECODING EMOTIONS

Tuning In to the Mind-Body Connection

Identifying the exact emotions you are experiencing at any given moment can sometimes be challenging. You know that you're feeling something but may not know exactly what. Thankfully, emotions are experienced throughout the entire body, so we can look to it for clues.

Our brain's limbic system governs our emotional responses and sends different chemical messages for the different emotions we experience. Our body has specific physical reactions to the various chemical messages, thus providing an indication as to the emotion that triggered them. For example, "stressed" is an emotional state that generally causes the release of extra adrenaline and cortisol. Those chemicals trigger physical reactions such as increased heart rate, changes in breathing, trembling, digestive upset, perspiration, and so on. If you're experiencing a combination of these symptoms, there's a good chance the emotion you're experiencing is "stressed."

Though there are some general reactions that give us a fairly predictable foundation, it's possible to experience multiple feelings simultaneously. For example, when we feel threatened, we often feel anger and fear at the same time. Additionally, physical responses to very different emotions can feel quite similar. For example, the physical indicators of being terrified and exhilarated are largely the same. The brain, in context with our individual experiences and beliefs, will shape which emotion we feel and how.

While the experience of emotions can be as varied as the people having them, the following chart provides some examples of physical indicators commonly associated with the emotions listed.

EMOTION	ASSOCIATED EMOTIONS	PHYSICAL INDICATOR	MENTAL OR EMOTIONAL INDICATOR
FEAR	ANXIOUS IRRITABLE PRIDEFUL JUDGMENTAL SCARCITY JEALOUS WEAK VULNERABLE CONTROLLING UNSAFE	rapid or shallow breathing, increased heart rate, blood draining from face or limbs, nausea, throat contraction, clenching or tightening in chest or stomach, sweaty palms, dizziness, butterflies or fluttering in stomach, muscle weakness	• UNSURE • UNEASINESS • RESTLESSNESS • HESITATION • PANIC • TERROR • PHOBIAS • APPREHENSION • PARANOIA • WORRY • INABILITY TO CONCENTRATE • DREAD • PREOCCUPATION WITH FUTURE EVENTS OR OTHER PEOPLE'S BEHAVIOR
HAPPINESS	CONTENT JOYFUL EXCITED OPTIMISTIC	warmth starting from the inside and radiating out, sometimes centered around chest, physical relaxation, or increased energy, feeling of expansiveness, breathing deeper, and easier mental clarity	• PLEASANT THOUGHTS AND FEELINGS • CONTENT • SATISFACTION • SAFETY • ELATION • POSITIVITY • ENTHUSIASM • VIBRANCY • BUOYANCY • CHEERFULNESS • SERENITY • SENSE OF WELL-BEING • HOPE

EMOTION	ASSOCIATED EMOTIONS	PHYSICAL INDICATOR	MENTAL OR EMOTIONAL INDICATOR
ANGER	FRUSTRATED RESENTFUL IRRITATION INCENSED RAGE HATRED	tightness of muscles, pain or pressure in back, neck, and jaw, feeling hot, adrenaline response including increased sensation in arms and hands, increased heart rate and blood pressure, shaking or trembling, sweating	• ESCALATION OF POWERFUL, INTENSE, OR SUPPRESSED FEELINGS • MASKING FEAR OR SADNESS • EXPLOSIVE OUTBURST • WITHDRAWN • SILENCE • DEFENSIVENESS OR BLAME • RESENTMENT • IRRITATION, SARCASM, OR CYNICISM
LOVE	PASSIONATE FOND FORGIVING COMPASSIONATE EMPATHETIC CARING	love can be a total physical experience, generally with increased blood flow and warmth often felt primarily in chest	• CONTENTMENT • STRONG AFFECTION • FEELING COMPLETE OR FILLED • COMPASSION • GENERAL WELL-BEING • BONDED • OBSERVANT • SELFLESS DESIRES AND ACTIONS
SADNESS	HURTING SORROWFUL LOSS GRIEVING LONELY	heaviness in chest, lump in throat, crying, aches and pains, lethargy and fatigue	• HEAVINESS • DOWN • BLUE • APATHY • BETRAYAL • ISOLATION OR ALONE • SORROW • ANGUISH • HOPELESSNESS OR DESPAIR

EMOTION	ASSOCIATED EMOTIONS	PHYSICAL INDICATOR	MENTAL OR EMOTIONAL INDICATOR
PEACEFUL	PRESENT GROUNDED CONTENT	relaxation in muscle tension, especially in face and upper torso, cessation or reduction of pain, warmth through body, reduced pulse, steady breathing	• CALMNESS • RELAXATION • PATIENCE • CONTENTMENT • CONNECTION • SERENITY • FLEXIBILITY • ACCEPTING • UNTROUBLED • PURPOSE
GUILT	SHAMEFUL REGRETFUL SELF-LOATHING	tightening or aching sensations in stomach and chest, or other uncomfortable sensations in head and face as well as lower abdomen	• FEAR • ANGER • SADNESS • REGRET • DESIRE TO RUN AWAY OR DISAPPEAR • AVOIDANCE OR DENIAL • EMBARRASSMENT • FEELING LIKE A FAILURE OR WORTHLESS
STRESS	OVERWHELMED UNSUPPORTED CONTROLLED OVERWORKED BURNED OUT OBLIGATED	muscle tension in shoulders, neck, and head, overly alert or difficulty concentrating, headaches, indigestion or nausea, rapid breathing, general aches and pains, heart palpitations, changes in eating and sleep habits	• FEELING PRESSURED BY PEOPLE OR CIRCUMSTANCES • DEPLETION • DRAINED • OVERWHELMED • BURDENED • ANXIOUS • FEAR • ANGER • SADNESS • HOPELESSNESS • NOTICEABLE CHANGES IN MOOD OR BEHAVIOR SUCH AS BEING REACTIVE, WITHDRAWN, INDECISIVE, IRRITABLE, TEARFUL, OR LASHING OUT

APPENDIX B

NEGATIVE EMOTIONS AND POSITIVE PROPERTIES

ESSENTIAL OIL	NEGATIVE EMOTIONS	POSITIVE PROPERTIES
SINGLE OILS		
ARBORVITAE	Overexerting Struggling Distant from God	Grace-filled Trusting Peaceful Surrender
BASIL	Fatigued Depleted Dependent	Energized Renewed Rested
BERGAMOT	Self-judgment Insecure Unloved	Self-acceptance Optimistic Confident
BIRCH	Unsupported Weak-willed Alienated	Supported Resolute Connected
BLUE TANSY	Procrastinating Resisting Apathetic	Inspired Initiative Motivated
BLACK PEPPER	Superficial Hiding Self-deception	Honest Authentic Courageous
CARDAMOM	Angry Aggressive Disrespectful	Objective Self-control Respectful
CASSIA	Fear of rejection Shy Timid	Courageous Unashamed Valued
CEDARWOOD	Separate Aloof Lonely	Connected Belonging Social
CILANTRO	Controlling Worried Trapped	Unattached Cleansing Liberated

ESSENTIAL OIL	NEGATIVE EMOTIONS	POSITIVE PROPERTIES
CINNAMON	Fear of rejection Sexual repression Pretense Jealousy	Attractive Healthy sexuality Intimate Accepting
CLARY SAGE	Confused Limited Blocked	Clarity Intuitive Imaginative
CLOVE	Controlled Self-betrayal Codependent Poor boundaries	Empowered Clear boundaries Protected
COPAIBA	Guilty Self-loathing Regretful	Forgiven Worthy Redefined
CORIANDER	Controlled Self-betrayal Disloyal	Integrity Inner guidance True to self
CUMIN	Unbridled ambition Self-centered Scarcity mindset	Balanced ambition Respectful Abundant thinking
CYPRESS	Rigid Perfectionistic Controlling	Trusting Flowing Adaptable
DILL	Bored Disinterested Overstimulated	Engaged Motivated Integration
DOUGLAS FIR	Repeating mistakes from the past Generational patterns Negative traditions	Wisdom Respectful Generational healing Healthy connections
EUCALYPTUS	Ill Depleted Despondent Defeated	Well Responsible Liberated
FENNEL	Irresponsible Loss of appetite Body neglect	Responsible Satiated In tune

ESSENTIAL OIL	NEGATIVE EMOTIONS	POSITIVE PROPERTIES
FRANKINCENSE	Darkness Deceived Spiritually disconnected Abandoned	Wisdom Discerning Spiritually connected
GERANIUM	Distrusting Grieving Brokenhearted	Trusting Loving Tolerant Open
GINGER	Victim mentality Blaming Powerless	Empowered Capable Responsible
GRAPEFRUIT	Body judgment Disrespecting body Obsession with food or dieting	Body acceptance Respect for body Meeting physical needs
HELICHRYSUM	Traumatized Wounded Hopeless	Whole Courageous Hopeful
JASMINE	Resistant Sexual fixation Sexual trauma	Intimate Pure Healthy sexuality
JUNIPER BERRY	Terrified Fearful Nightmares	Protected Courageous Dreaming
KUMQUAT	Inauthentic Passive aggressive Hiding	Authentic Honest Sincere
LAVENDER	Blocked communication Hiding Constricted	Expressive Open Calm
LEMON	Unfocused Fatigued Difficulty learning	Focused Energized Alert
LEMONGRASS	Despairing Hoarding Lethargic	Clarity Simplicity Cleansing

ESSENTIAL OIL	NEGATIVE EMOTIONS	POSITIVE PROPERTIES
LITSEA	Limited Stifled Blocked	Manifesting Inspired Aligned
LIME	Disinterested Despairing Resigned Apathetic	Engaged Courageous Determined Grateful
MANUKA	Abandoned Wounded Unsafe	Upheld Comforted Shielded
MARJORAM	Isolated Fear of rejection Cold Distrust	Connected Warm Loving
MELALEUCA	Boundary violation Enmeshed Self-betrayal	Energetic boundaries Respectful connections Resilient
MELISSA	Burdened Misaligned Darkness	Joyful Integrity Enlightened
MYRRH	Distrusting Ungrounded Unsafe in the world	Safe Secure Trusting Nurtured
NEROLI	Unfulfilled Resentful Aloof	Committed Kind Intimate
OREGANO	Prideful Willful Opinionated	Humble Willing Nonattachment
PATCHOULI	Obsessive Disconnected Body shame	Moderation Balanced Body connection
PEPPERMINT	Heavyhearted Pessimistic Dejected	Buoyant Optimistic Relieved

ESSENTIAL OIL	NEGATIVE EMOTIONS	POSITIVE PROPERTIES
PETITGRAIN	Inherited limitations Dishonoring Unhealthy traditions	Chain-breaking Pioneering Healthy family connections
RED MANDARIN	Burdened parenting Exhausted Unappreciated	Fulfilled parenting Refreshed Cherished
ROMAN CHAMOMILE	Purposeless Directionless Unsettled	Purposeful Guided Peaceful
ROSE	Unloved Wounded Disheartened	Loved Compassionate Healing
ROSEMARY	Confused Ignorant Uncertain	Mental clarity Knowledgeable Teachable
SANDALWOOD	Prideful Materialistic Distracted	Humble Devotion Spiritual
SIBERIAN FIR	Regretful Loss Fretting	Perspective Wisdom Adapting
SPEARMINT	Inarticulate Timid Withholding voice	Clarity Confident Articulate
SPIKENARD	Ungrateful Victim mentality Resisting	Grateful Acceptance Content
TANGERINE	Overburdened Overworked Stifled	Cheerful Spontaneous Creative
THYME	Unforgiving Intolerant Angry Resentful	Forgiving Tolerant Patient Understanding

ESSENTIAL OIL	NEGATIVE EMOTIONS	POSITIVE PROPERTIES
VETIVER	Scattered Ungrounded Avoiding	Centered Grounded Present
WHITE FIR	Codependent Destructive patterns Generational burdens	Free Healthy patterns Generational healing
WILD ORANGE	Scarcity Serious Rigid	Abundant Sense of humor Playful
WINTERGREEN	Controlling Self-reliant Willful	Surrender Relying on the Divine Letting go
YLANG YLANG	Sadness Joyless Overanalyzing	Freedom Playful Intuitive
OILS BLENDS		
ANTI-AGING BLEND	Discouragement Spiritual blindness Spiritually disconnected	Hopeful Transforming Trust in the Divine
CELLULAR BLEND	Broken Immobilized Powerless	Repairing Balanced Rebirth Transforming
CLEANSING BLEND	Trapped Negative Toxic	Unencumbered Purifying Clean
COMFORTING BLEND	Grieving Loss Traumatized	Comforted Whole Serene
DETOXIFICATION BLEND	Dependent Toxic habits Self-sabotage Apathetic	Revitalized Unrestricted Clear

ESSENTIAL OIL	NEGATIVE EMOTIONS	POSITIVE PROPERTIES
DIGESTIVE BLEND	Unenthusiastic Undernourished Overstimulated	Enthusiastic Nourished Assimilation
ENCOURAGING BLEND	Unmotivated Gloomy Weary	Motivated Encouraged Energized
FOCUS BLEND	Distracted Procrastinating Overactive	Focused Commited Present
GROUNDING BLEND	Ungrounded Disconnected Scattered	Grounded Connected Stable
HOLIDAY BLEND	Estranged Stressed Cold	Connected Celebratory Warm
HOPE BLEND	Despairing Traumatized Shameful	Hopeful Healing Rebirth
INSPIRING BLEND	Lack of confidence Regimented Joyless	Passionate Risk-taking Spontaneous
INVIGORATING BLEND	Stifled Blocked creativity Unmotivated	Invigorated Creative Motivated
JOYFUL BLEND	Despairing Discouraged Heavyhearted	Bright Joyful Carefree
MASSAGE BLEND	Tense Stressed Rigid	Relaxed Balanced Flexible

ESSENTIAL OIL	NEGATIVE EMOTIONS	POSITIVE PROPERTIES
METABOLIC BLEND	Worthless Critical Strict	Worthy Acceptance Beautiful
MONTHLY BLEND	Invulnerable Suffering Guarded	Vulnerable Serene Receptive
OUTDOOR BLEND	Poor boundaries Attacked Defenseless	Boundaries Safe Self-contained
PROTECTIVE BLEND	Attacked Unprotected Controlled	Protected Capable Independent
REASSURING BLEND	Anxious Controlling Attached Afraid	Peaceful Content Still Serene
RENEWING BLEND	Unforgiving Critical Resentful	Forgiving Understanding Tolerant
RESPIRATORY BLEND	Unloved Sad Constricted Grieving	Loved Cared for Receiving Solace
RESTFUL BLEND	Stressed Restless Disconnected	Calm Tranquil Compassionate
SOOTHING BLEND	Resisting Pained Panicked	Strengthened Soothed Serene
SUNSHINE BLEND	Stagnant Stressed Cynical	Spontaneous Carefree Optimistic
TENSION BLEND	Imbalanced Burned out Tense	Equilibrium Calm Relieved

ESSENTIAL OIL	NEGATIVE EMOTIONS	POSITIVE PROPERTIES
TOPICAL BLEND	Self-critical Suppressed anger Inadequate	Self-acceptance Worthwhile Ample
UPLIFTING BLEND	Pessimistic Burdened Heavyhearted Hopeless	Cheerful Uplifted Hopeful
WOMEN'S BLEND	Resisting femininity Overly masculine Repressed sexuality	Accepting femininity Soft Healthy sexual expression

APPENDIX C
EMOTIONS INDEX

A

Abandoned: Frankincense, Myrrh, Marjoram, Geranium, Manuka

Abundant: Wild Orange, Spikenard, Invigorating Blend, Joyful Blend, Tangerine, Cumin, Litsea

Abuse: Cinnamon, Clove, Helichrysum, White Fir, Douglas Fir, Jasmine

Acceptance: Rose, Bergamot, Ylang Ylang, Spikenard, Jasmine

Accountable: (see *Responsible*)

Adaptable: Women's Blend, Cypress, Siberian Fir

Adjusting: Rosemary, Detoxification Blend, Digestive Blend

Afraid: (see *Fearful*)

Agitated: (see *Irritated*)

Alienated: Birch, Cedarwood, Myrrh

Aloof: Marjoram, Grounding Blend, Jasmine, Neroli

Ambitious, overly: Cumin, Arborvitae, Oregano

Angry: Cardamom, Thyme, Geranium, Ylang Ylang, Spikenard, White Fir, Renewing Blend, Topical Blend

Anguished: Helichrysum, Melissa, Copaiba

Annoyed: Renewing Blend, Cardamom

Anxious: Basil, Tension Blend, Comforting Blend, Restful Blend

Apathetic: Lemongrass, Vetiver, Lime, Detoxification Blend, Blue Tansy

Appetite, loss of: Digestive Blend, Fennel

Apprehensive: Cassia, Cinnamon, Melissa

Approval, need for: Bergamot

Approved of: Rose, Bergamot

Argumentative: Lavender, Cardamom, Oregano

Arrogant: Oregano

Ashamed: (see *Shameful*)

Assertive: Clove, Black Pepper

Attacked: Protective Blend, Outdoor Blend, Birch

Attachments, negative: Oregano, Sandalwood, Spikenard, Lemongrass

Attentive: Lemon

Authentic: Wild Orange, Cassia, Spearmint, Black Pepper, Kumquat

Avoiding: Soothing Blend, Vetiver, Helichrysum, Grounding Blend, Juniper Berry, Jasmine

B

Balanced: Petitgrain, Patchouli, Massage Blend, Cellular Blend, Holiday Blend

Barriers, emotional: Marjoram, Monthly Blend, Rose

Believing: (see *Faith*)

Belittled: Bergamot, Metabolic Blend

Belonging: Cedarwood, Marjoram

Bereaved: (see *Grieving*)

Betrayed: Geranium, Rose, Ylang Ylang

Bitter: Thyme, Renewing Blend, Neroli

Blaming others: Ginger, Spikenard, Cardamom, Vetiver, Renewing Blend, Topical Blend, Neroli

Blaming self: Bergamot, Clove, Copaiba

Blocked: Cypress, Thyme, Oregano, Litsea

Body acceptance: Grapefruit, Patchouli, Cinnamon, Fennel, Digestive Blend, Metabolic Blend

Body shame: Patchouli, Grapefruit, Cinnamon, Metabolic Blend, Jasmine

Body tension: Tension Blend, Massage Blend, Patchouli

Bonding: Geranium, Marjoram, Myrrh, Cedarwood, Monthly Blend, Douglas Fir

Bored: Dill

Boundaries: Protective Blend, Melaleuca, Clove, Outdoor Blend, Oregano, Holiday Blend

Brave: (see *Courageous*)

Buoyant: (see *Joyful*)

Burdened: White Fir, Wintergreen, Tangerine, Douglas Fir, Cilantro, Melissa, Red Mandarin, Manuka, Anti-Aging Blend, Sunshine Blend, Cellular Blend, Comforting Blend, Inspiring Blend

Burned out: Basil, Tension Blend, Respiratory Blend

C

Calm: Lavender, Patchouli, Roman Chamomile, Sandalwood, Massage Blend, Restful Blend, Tension Blend, Grounding Blend, Focus Blend, Neroli

Capable: Clove, Cassia, Ginger, Protective Blend

Cared for: Respiratory Blend, Rose, Manuka

Carefree: Joyful Blend, Sunshine Blend

Careless: (see *Apathetic*)

Centered: Vetiver, Roman Chamomile

Chain-breaking: Petitgrain

Change, resisting: Cilantro, Blue Tansy, Detoxification Blend

Chaotic: Lemon, Vetiver

Charitable: Wild Orange, Spikenard, Rose

Cheerful: Tangerine, Lime, Wild Orange, Invigorating Blend,
Joyful Blend, Uplifting Blend

Childish: (see *Immature*)

Childlike: Ylang Ylang, Invigorating Blend, Geranium, Wild Orange,
Tangerine, Sunshine Blend, Red Mandarin

Clarity, mental: Lemon, Rosemary, Spearmint, Dill, Peppermint,
Grounding Blend, Soothing Blend, Focus Blend

Clarity, spiritual: Clary Sage, Frankincense, Sandalwood, Lemongrass,
Copaiba

Cleansing: Cleansing Blend, Lemongrass, Bergamot, Frankincense,
Detoxification Blend, Cilantro

Clear-minded: (see *Clarity, mental*)

Clingy: Eucalyptus, Ylang Ylang, Cilantro

Closed, emotionally: Respiratory Blend, Ylang Ylang, Monthly Blend,
Rose, Geranium, Jasmine, Holiday Blend

Closed-minded: Rosemary, Oregano, Wild Orange, Lemon,
Digestive Blend, Coriander

Codependent: Melaleuca, Clove, Protective Blend, Cleansing Blend, Oregano, Ginger, White Fir, Jasmine, Outdoor Blend

Comforted: Respiratory Blend, Massage Blend, Geranium, Joyful Blend, Tension Blend, Manuka, Comforting Blend, Soothing Blend, Uplifting Blend, Siberian Fir

Committed: Ginger, Coriander, Grounding Blend, Blue Tansy, Neroli

Communication: Lavender, Spearmint

Compassionate: Rose, Restful Blend, Geranium

Competitive: Oregano, Cumin

Composed: Patchouli, Soothing Blend

Confident: Bergamot, Cassia, Roman Chamomile, Spearmint, Lavender, Invigorating Blend, Patchouli, Outdoor Blend, Metabolic Blend, Encouraging Blend

Conforming: Coriander, Clove, Ginger, Cassia

Confused: Clary Sage, Lemon, Peppermint, Rosemary

Connected, emotionally: Marjoram, Vetiver, Cedarwood, Geranium, Birch, Lime, Ylang Ylang, Women's Blend, Holiday Blend

Connected, mentally: (see *Clarity, mental*)

Connected, physically: Patchouli, Grounding Blend, Jasmine

Connected, spiritually: Frankincense, Melissa, Roman Chamomile, Sandalwood, Spikenard, Rose, Reassuring Blend, Manuka

Consciousness, higher: Sandalwood, Joyful Blend, Helichrysum, Frankincense

Considerate: Cumin, Renewing Blend

Consoled: (see *Comforted*)

Constricted: Lavender, Cypress, Respiratory Blend, Cilantro, Rose

Content: Spikenard, Comforting Blend, Reassuring Blend

Contentious: Renewing Blend, Thyme

Controlled: Protective Blend, Clove, Coriander, Ginger

Controlling: Cilantro, Cleansing Blend, Cinnamon, Wintergreen, Cypress, Sandalwood, Metabolic Blend, Arborvitae, Reassuring Blend

Cooperative: Neroli, Cumin

Courageous: Helichrysum, Birch, Cassia, Clove, Ginger, Outdoor Blend, Joyful Blend, Juniper Berry, Lime, Spearmint, Black Pepper, Respiratory Blend, Hope Blend

Creative: Wild Orange, Tangerine, Invigorating Blend, Clary Sage, Inspiring Blend

Creativity, blocked: Invigorating Blend, Tangerine, Wild Orange, Clary Sage

Crisis: Lavender, Basil, Peppermint, Geranium, Vetiver

Critical: Bergamot, Metabolic Blend, Thyme, Renewing Blend

Cynical: (see *Pessimistic*)

D

Dark night of the soul: Melissa, Frankincense, Helichrysum, Anti-Aging Blend, Hope Blend

Dark, fear of the: Juniper Berry

Darkness, spiritual: Lemongrass, Frankincense, Melaleuca, Clary Sage, Melissa, Joyful Blend, Sandalwood

Death, acceptance of: Roman Chamomile, Frankincense, Spikenard

Deceived: Clary Sage, Frankincense

Decisive: Lemon, Clove

Defeated: Clove, Invigorating Blend, Eucalyptus, Ginger, Fennel

Defenseless: Outdoor Blend, Protective Blend

Defensive: Oregano, Ylang Ylang, Geranium, Holiday Blend

Defiant: Oregano, Ylang Ylang

Degraded: Bergamot, Clove

Dejected: (see *Despairing*)

Denial: (see *Avoiding*)

Dependent: Melaleuca, Clove, Ginger, Jasmine

Depleted: Basil, Peppermint, Melaleuca, Tension Blend, Massage Blend, Uplifting Blend

Desire, lack of: Grounding Blend, Fennel, Black Pepper, Invigorating Blend, Lemongrass, Jasmine

Despairing: Joyful Blend, Melissa, Bergamot, Respiratory Blend, Eucalyptus, Lemongrass, Peppermint, Helichrysum, Lime, Hope Blend, Siberian Fir

Despondent: Lemongrass, Melissa, Eucalyptus, Invigorating Blend, Vetiver

Determined: Helichrysum, Lime, Joyful Blend, Uplifting Blend

Dieting, obsessed with: Grapefruit, Bergamot, Detoxification Blend, Vetiver, Patchouli, Fennel, Metabolic Blend, Digestive Blend

Discerning: Clary Sage, Frankincense, Lemongrass, Litsea

Disconnected, emotionally: Thyme, Fennel, Vetiver, Ylang Ylang, Holiday Blend

Disconnected, mentally: (see *Clarity, mental*)

Disconnected, physically: Patchouli, Grounding Blend, Vetiver, Jasmine

Disconnected, spiritually: Frankincense, Sandalwood, Clary Sage,

Rose, Manuka, Anti-Aging Blend, Reassuring Blend

Discontent: Spikenard, Wild Orange

Discouraged: Lime, Melissa, Joyful Blend, Wild Orange, Roman Chamomile, Red Mandarin, Anti-Aging Blend, Cellular Blend, Encouraging Blend, Invigorating Blend

Disheartened: (see *Heavyhearted*)

Dishonest: Black Pepper, Vetiver, Cassia, Lavender, Geranium

Disinterested: Dill

Disengaged: Dill, Invigorating Blend, Lemon

Distant: Marjoram, Cedarwood, Jasmine, Birch, Holiday Blend

Distracted: Focus Blend, Litsea, Lemon

Distraught: Respiratory Blend

Distrusting: Geranium, Marjoram, Myrrh, Respiratory Blend, Jasmine, Arborvitae

Dominated: Clove, Protective Blend, Outdoor Blend, Ginger

Doubtful: Sandalwood

Drained: (see *Depleted*)

Dreaming: Juniper Berry, Melissa

Drudgery: Roman Chamomile, Coriander, Invigorating Blend, Fennel, Tangerine, Sunshine Blend

Dull: Invigorating Blend, Wild Orange, Roman Chamomile, Inspiring Blend, Sunshine Blend

Dumb: (see *Incapable*)

Duty-bound: Tangerine, Petitgrain, Inspiring Blend

E

Eating issues: (see *Dieting, obsession with*)

Egotistical: Oregano

Elevated: Joyful Blend, Lime, Melissa

Embarrassed: Cassia, Jasmine

Empathetic: Geranium, Rose, Renewing Blend, Neroli, Monthly Blend

Empathetic, overly: (see *Boundaries*)

Empowered: Ginger, Clove, Melaleuca

Emptiness: Vetiver, Sandalwood

Encouraged: Melissa, Lime, Eucalyptus, Joyful Blend, Wild Orange, Encouraging Blend

Energized: Lime, Basil, Lemon, Detoxification Blend, Melissa, Encouraging Blend, Blue Tansy

Energy, lack of: Lemon, Peppermint, Wild Orange, Joyful Blend, Invigorating Blend

Engaged: Dill, Lime, Digestive Blend

Enlightened: Melissa, Frankincense, Sandalwood, Rosemary

Enmeshed: Melaleuca, Clove, Protective Blend, Oregano

Enthusiastic: Melissa, Digestive Blend, Sunshine Blend

Envious: (See *Jealous*)

Escapism: Vetiver, Patchouli, Grounding Blend, Eucalyptus, Jasmine, Neroli

Estranged: (see *Separated*)

Exasperated: Basil, Lavender

Excessive: Grounding Blend, Sandalwood, Arborvitae, Oregano, Jasmine, Cumin

Exhausted: Basil, Invigorating Blend, Tension Blend, Respiratory Blend, Red Mandarin, Encouraging Blend, Blue Tansy

Expressive: Lavender, Spearmint, Topical Blend, Invigorating Blend

F

Façade: Black Pepper, Kumquat, Vetiver, Soothing Blend, Helichrysum, Cinnamon, Juniper Berry

Failing: Bergamot, Roman Chamomile, Cumin

Faith: Sandalwood, Anti-Aging Blend, Hope Blend, Uplifting Blend

Family traditions: (see *Generational Healing*)

Father, connection to: Frankincense

Fatigued, mentally: Lemon, Rosemary, Dill, Tension Blend

Fatigued, physically: (see *Exhausted*)

Fearful: Juniper Berry, Cassia, Cinnamon, Birch, Cypress, Lavender, Myrrh, Spikenard, Peppermint, Soothing Blend, Cumin, Reassuring Blend

Fearless: (see *Courageous*)

Firm: Clove, Birch

Flexible: Cypress, Massage Blend, Wild Orange, Birch, Oregano

Flighty: (see *Ungrounded*)

Focused: Lemon, Rosemary, Spearmint, Grounding Blend, Focus Blend

Food, preoccupation with: (see *Dieting, obsession with*)

Foolish: Cassia

Forgetful: Lemon, Peppermint

Forgiven: Copaiba, Siberian Fir, Geranium, Red Mandarin

Forgiving: Geranium, Thyme, Renewing Blend, Siberian Fir

Frantic: (see *Hurried*)

Friendless: Marjoram, Cedarwood, Birch

Frustrated: Geranium, Cardamom, Neroli, Roman Chamomile

Fulfilled: Roman Chamomile, Tangerine, Jasmine, Neroli

G

Generational healing: White Fir, Douglas Fir, Petitgrain

Generational issues: White Fir, Petitgrain, Birch, Douglas Fir, Jasmine, Cellular Blend

Generous: Wild Orange

Gentle: Geranium, Ylang Ylang, Women's Blend

Giving up: Hope Blend, Helichrysum, Soothing Blend

Good enough: (see *Worthy*)

Grace: Arborvitae, Rose, Frankincense, Wintergreen, Anti-Aging Blend, Manuka

Grateful: Spikenard, Wild Orange, Helichrysum, Tension Blend, Douglas Fir, Lime, Manuka

Greedy: Wild Orange, Spikenard

Grieving: Respiratory Blend, Soothing Blend, Geranium, Lime, Ylang Ylang, Massage Blend, Manuka, Comforting Blend, Siberian Fir

Grounded: Grounding Blend, Birch, Patchouli, Vetiver, Arborvitae, Myrrh, Focus Blend

Guarded: Monthly Blend, Jasmine

Guilty: Copaiba, Bergamot, Lemon, Peppermint

H

Harassed: (see *Attacked*)

Hardened: Rose, Geranium, Ylang Ylang, Tangerine, Jasmine

Hardhearted: Rose, Geranium, Thyme

Harsh: Marjoram, Geranium, Cardamom

Hate: Thyme, Cleansing Blend, Cardamom

Haunted: Frankincense, Protective Blend, Melissa

Healing: Helichrysum, Geranium, Eucalyptus, Respiratory Blend, Jasmine, Rose, Ylang Ylang, Soothing Blend, Manuka, Hope Blend, Comforting Blend

Healthy: Cellular Blend, Eucalyptus, Basil

Heard: Lavender, Spearmint

Heartbroken: Geranium, Rose

Heartless: Rose, Geranium

Heavyhearted: Lime, Joyful Blend, Geranium, Tangerine, Peppermint, Rose, Uplifting Blend

Helpless: Clove, Ginger, Protective Blend, Uplifting Blend

Hereditary issues: (see *Generational issues*)

Hesitant: (see *Indecisive*)

Hiding: Cassia, Black Pepper, Lavender, Spearmint, Grapefruit, Juniper Berry, White Fir, Kumquat

Hoarding: Lemongrass, Cleansing Blend, Detoxification Blend, Wild Orange

Holding back: Cassia, Lavender, Spearmint, Jasmine

Holding onto past: Thyme, Lemongrass, Cleansing Blend, Detoxification Blend, Wintergreen, Siberian Fir

Honest: Black Pepper, Geranium, Lavender, Lime, Kumquat, Siberian Fir

Hopeful: Melissa, Lime, Bergamot, Helichrysum, Anti-Aging Blend, Encouraging Blend, Hope Blend, Uplifting Blend

Hopeless: Hope Blend, Melissa, Clary Sage, Bergamot, Helichrysum, Lime, Uplifting Blend

Humiliated: Cassia

Humble: Oregano, Sandalwood

Humor, sense of: Wild Orange, Joyful Blend, Ylang Ylang, Sunshine Blend

Hurried: Massage Blend, Tension Blend, Restful Blend

Hurtful: Renewing Blend, Rose, Thyme

Hypocritical: Kumquat, Clary Sage, Frankincense, Black Pepper

Hysterical: (see *Panicked*)

I

Illness, attached to: Eucalyptus, Patchouli

Imbalanced: Restful Blend, Invigorating Blend, Tension Blend

Immature: Geranium, Fennel

Immobilized: (see *Stuck*)

Impatient: Grounding Blend, Thyme, Neroli

Impoverished: Wild Orange, Spikenard

Imprisoned: (see *Trapped*)

Impulsive: Sandalwood, Vetiver, Jasmine

Inadequate: Bergamot, Metabolic Blend

Inauthentic: Kumquat, Black Pepper

Incapable: Bergamot, Lemon, Peppermint, Rosemary, Cassia

Inconsiderate: Cinnamon, Renewing Blend, Spikenard, Cumin

Inconsistent: Grounding Blend, Coriander

Indecisive: Lemon, Peppermint

Independent: Protective Blend, Clove

Indifferent: (see *Apathetic*)

Inferior: Bergamot

Inflexible: (see *Rigid*)

Initiative: Blue Tansy

Innocent: Ylang Ylang, Geranium, Jasmine, Red Mandarin

Insecure: Cassia, Bergamot, Cinnamon, Lemon, Invigorating Blend

Insensitive: Cumin, Oregano

Insignificant: Roman Chamomile

Inspired: Inspiring Blend, Roman Chamomile, Lemon, Rosemary, Citrus Blend, Joyful Blend, Blue Tansy

Instability: Grounding Blend

Integration: Dill

Integrity: Coriander, Black Pepper, Melissa, Protective Blend, Kumquat

Intimate: (see *Sexuality, healthy*)

Intimidated: Clove, Outdoor Blend, Ginger

Intolerant: Geranium, Rose, Thyme, Cardamom, Renewing Blend

Introvert: Marjoram, Cedarwood

Intuitive: Clary Sage, Litsea, Blue Tansy

Invigorated: Peppermint, Lemon, Invigorating Blend

Invulnerable: Monthly Blend, Marjoram

Irrational: Cardamom, Juniper Berry, Soothing Blend

Irresponsible: Fennel, Ginger, Grounding Blend

Irritated: Renewing Blend, Women's Blend

Isolated: Marjoram, Cedarwood, Myrrh

J

Jaded: Red Mandarin, Spikenard

Jealous: Cinnamon, Wild Orange, Sandalwood, Oregano

Joyful: Lemon, Lime, Wild Orange, Tangerine, Peppermint, Ylang Ylang, Invigorating Blend, Joyful Blend, Melissa, Red Mandarin, Holiday Blend, Uplifting Blend, Sunshine Blend

Joyless: Joyful Blend, Lemon, Ylang Ylang, Tangerine, Melissa, Red Mandarin, Inspiring Blend, Uplifting Blend

Judged: Birch, Clove, Ginger, Cassia

Judgmental: Geranium, Rose, Black Pepper, Renewing Blend

K

Kind: Geranium, Women's Blend, Neroli

Know-it-all: Oregano, Wintergreen, Sandalwood

L

Learning issues: Lemon, Rosemary, Digestive Blend

Left out: (see *Isolated*)

Lethargic: Lemongrass, Invigorating Blend, Blue Tansy

Liberated: Detoxification Blend, Cleansing Blend, Lavender, Melissa, Eucalyptus, Cilantro

Lighthearted: (see *Joyful*)

Limiting beliefs: Detoxification Blend, Lemongrass, Bergamot, Vetiver, Litsea

Lonely: Marjoram, Cedarwood, Frankincense, Myrrh

Loss: Geranium, Ylang Ylang, Comforting Blend, Siberian Fir

Loss of will to live: Hope Blend, Invigorating Blend, Melissa, Frankincense, Lime, Joyful Blend

Lost: (see *Purposeless*)

Loving: Rose, Geranium, Marjoram, Renewing Blend

Loved: Frankincense, Rose, Respiratory Blend, Myrrh, Bergamot, Marjoram, Manuka

Loyal: Petitgrain, Jasmine, Neroli

Lustful: Cinnamon, Jasmine

M

Mad: (see *Angry*)

Manifesting: Litsea

Manipulated: Clove, Protective Blend

Manipulative: Cinnamon

Masculine, overly: Women's Blend, Monthly Blend

Materialistic: Sandalwood, Oregano, Cilantro, Detoxification Blend

Mean: Geranium, Ylang Ylang, Neroli

Melancholy: (see *Sad*)

Menopause, dread of: Monthly Blend, Grapefruit, Jasmine

Menstruation, dread of: Monthly Blend, Grapefruit, Jasmine

Moderation: Patchouli

Moods, unstable: Joyful Blend

Mother, connection to: Myrrh, Women's Blend, Monthly Blend

Motivated: Invigorating Blend, Black Pepper, Dill, Encouraging Blend, Blue Tansy

N

Narrow-minded: (see *Closed-minded*)

Negative habits: Detoxification Blend

Neglected: Myrrh, Cedarwood, Marjoram

Nervous: Basil, Wild Orange, Tension Blend, Spearmint

Nightmares: Juniper Berry

Nonattachment: Oregano, Sandalwood, Cilantro, Wintergreen, Lemongrass, Spikenard, Cumin

Nourished: Grapefruit, Myrrh, Digestive Blend

Numb: Fennel

Nurtured: Myrrh, Rose, Frankincense, Geranium, Ylang Ylang, Monthly Blend

O

Objective: Cardamom, Thyme

Obsessed: Patchouli, Detoxification Blend, Bergamot, Frankincense, Joyful Blend, Peppermint, Vetiver, White Fir, Douglas Fir, Jasmine, Basil, Grapefruit

Obsessive-compulsive: Cilantro, Cypress, Reassuring Blend, Bergamot, Sandalwood, Black Pepper, Cleansing Blend, Jasmine

Offended: (see *Unforgiving*)

Open-minded: Clary Sage, Wild Orange, Massage Blend, Rosemary, Thyme

Opinionated: Oregano

Oppressed: Clove, Protective Blend, White Fir

Optimistic: Melissa, Invigorating Blend, Tangerine, Bergamot, Peppermint, Joyful Blend, Sunshine Blend, Siberian Fir

Out of control: Grounding Blend, Ginger, Jasmine

Overanalyzing: Wild Orange, Ylang Ylang, Sandalwood, Basil

Overstimulated: Digestive Blend, Grounding Blend, Dill

Overthinking: (see *Overanalyzing*)

Overwhelmed: Basil, Massage Blend, Tension Blend, Digestive Blend, Tangerine, Melissa, Red Mandarin, Restful Blend

Overworked: (see *Workaholic*)

P

Pain, emotional: Helichrysum, Hope Blend, Manuka, Soothing Blend, Geranium, Peppermint, Comforting Blend, Topical Blend

Pain, resisting: Soothing Blend, Helichrysum, Vetiver

Panicked: Grounding Blend, Soothing Blend

Passionate: Jasmine, Fennel, Inspiring Blend

Passive-agressive: Kumquat, Cilantro

Patient: Grounding Blend, Thyme, Neroli, Renewing Blend, Restful Blend

Peaceful: Reassuring Blend, Restful Blend, Roman Chamomile, Patchouli, Copaiba, Siberian Fir

Peer pressure: (see *Controlled*)

Perfectionistic: Cypress, Restful Blend, Sunshine Blend

Persecuted: (see *Attacked*)

Persevering: Helichrysum, Grounding Blend, Hope Blend

Perspective: Siberian Fir, Red Mandarin, Frankincense, Clary Sage

Pessimistic: Spikenard, Wild Orange, Peppermint, Tangerine, Renewing Blend, Sunshine Blend

Pioneering: Petitgrain

Playful: Ylang Ylang, Wild Orange, Tangerine, Joyful Blend, Inspiring Blend, Sunshine Blend

Poor, financially: (see *Impoverished*)

Possessive: Sandalwood, Oregano, Wintergreen

Powerless: Clove, Ginger, Jasmine, Manuka, Present: Focus Blend, Ginger, Lemon, Patchouli, Siberian Fir, Vetiver, Grounding Blend

Present: Focus Blend, Ginger, Lemon, Patchouli, Siberian Fir, Vetiver, Grounding Blend

Pretense: (see *Superficial*)

Prideful: Oregano, Sandalwood, Wintergreen, Black Pepper

Proactive: Clove, Fennel

Procrastinating: Blue Tansy, Focus Blend

Protected: Protective Blend, Clove, Outdoor Blend, Frankincense, Juniper Berry

Purifying: Cleansing Blend, Lemongrass, Jasmine, Detoxification Blend

Purposeful: Roman Chamomile, Ginger, Blue Tansy, Copaiba, Litsea

Purposeless: Roman Chamomile, Frankincense

Q

Quarrelsome: (see *Argumentative*)

Quick-tempered: Geraniumm, Cardamom

Quitting: Helichrysum, Hope Blend

R

Rage: Cardamom, Thyme, Cleansing Blend

Rational: Lemon, Cardamom, Dill

Rebelling: Copaiba

Rebirth: Cellular Blend, Helichrysum, Hope Blend

Reclusive: Marjoram, Cedarwood

Refreshed: (see *Renewed*)

Regretful: Copaiba, Siberian Fir

Rejection: Lavender, Cinnamon, Lime, Clove, Marjoram, Monthly Blend, Litsea

Relationships: Neroli, Melaleuca, Protective Blend, Oregano, Jasmine, Geranium, Marjoram, Cedarwood

Relaxed: Tension Blend, Restful Blend, Lavender, Roman Chamomile, Massage Blend, Arborvitae, Joyful Blend

Relieved: Helichrysum, Tension Blend, Peppermint

Renewed: Basil, Peppermint, Red Mandarin

Repressed: Lavender, Vetiver, Black Pepper, Jasmine, Kumquat, Ylang Ylang

Resentful: Geranium, Thyme, Renewing Blend, Neroli

Resigned: (see *Despairing*)

Resilient: Melaleuca, Helichrysum, Lime, Soothing Blend, Neroli, Copaiba

Resisting: Vetiver, Soothing Blend, Spikenard, Digestive Blend, Fennel, Women's Blend

Resolute: Birch, Spearmint

Respectful: Cardamom, Douglas Fir, Melaleuca, Cumin

Responsible: Ginger, Fennel, Grounding Blend, Eucalyptus, Blue Tansy

Restless: Restful Blend, Comforting Blend, Neroli, Lavender

Revitalized: (see *Energized*)

Rigid: Cypress, Oregano, Wild Orange, Tangerine, Massage Blend

Rushed: (see *Hurried*)

S

Sacrificing: Sandalwood, Wintergreen, Arborvitae

Sad: Respiratory Blend, Ylang Ylang, Geranium, Peppermint, Massage Blend, Joyful Blend, Siberian Fir

Safe: Myrrh, Frankincense, Lavender, Respiratory Blend, Protective Blend, Melaleuca, Manuka, Holiday Blend, Outdoor Blend

Scarcity: Wild Orange, Spikenard, Cumin

Scattered: Vetiver, Grounding Blend, Spearmint, Focus Blend

Secure: (see *Protected*)

Self, true to: Coriander, Lavender, Birch, Black Pepper, Clove, Protective Blend, Kumquat

Self, weak sense of: Bergamot, Vetiver, Ginger, Grounding Blend, Fennel, Jasmine

Self-acceptance: Bergamot, Grapefruit, Metabolic Blend, Lemon, Jasmine, Patchouli, Hope Blend, Topical Blend

Self-assured: (see *Confident*)

Self-aware: Juniper Berry, Topical Blend, Copaiba, Kumquat

Self-betrayal: Coriander

Self-centered: Cumin

Self-control: Cardamom, Thyme, Oregano, Metabolic Blend, Ginger, Soothing Blend

Self-critical: Metabolic Blend, Bergamot, Litsea

Self-deception: Black Pepper

Self-doubt: (see *Self-esteem*)

Self-esteem: Bergamot, Metabolic Blend, Cassia, Jasmine, Litsea

Self-expression: Lavender, Invigorating Blend, Spearmint, Jasmine

Self-judgment: Bergamot, Metabolic Blend, Lemon, Topical Blend

Self-punishing: Bergamot, Metabolic Blend, Jasmine

Self-sabotage: Metabolic Blend, Detoxification Blend, Blue Tansy, Majoram

Selfish: Spikenard

Sensitive, overly: Outdoor Blend, Protective Blend, Clove, Ginger, Holiday Blend

Separated: Myrrh, Frankincense, Cedarwood, Manuka

Serious, overly: Tangerine, Invigorating Blend, Joyful Blend, Wild Orange, Inspiring Blend, Sunshine Blend

Sexual fixation: (see *Sexuality, imbalanced*)

Sexual identity: Cinnamon

Sexual trauma: Jasmine, Helichrysum, Hope Blend

Sexuality, repressed: (see *Sexuality, imbalanced*)

Sexuality, healthy: Cinnamon, Women's Blend, Patchouli, Jasmine, Neroli

Sexuality, imbalanced: Cinnamon, Women's Blend, Jasmine, Neroli

Shameful: Copaiba, Bergamot, Frankincense, Fennel, Cassia, Jasmine, Hope Blend

Shock: Basil, Peppermint, Wintergreen

Shy: Cassia, Spearmint, Cinnamon, Ginger

Sincere: Kumquat, Black Pepper

Sleep, disrupted: Juniper Berry, Massage Blend

Soothed: (see *Comforted*)

Speaking, fear of: Spearmint, Lavender

Spiritual: Frankincense, Arborvitae, Manuka, Sandalwood, Rose, Roman Chamomile, Anti-Aging Blend

Spiritual blindness: Anti-Aging Blend, Clary Sage, Lemongrass, Frankincense

Spontaneous: Wild Orange, Invigorating Blend, Tangerine, Inspiring Blend, Sunshine Blend

Stable: Grounding Blend, Patchouli, Monthly Blend, Joyful Blend

Stagnant: (see *Stuck*)

Stern: (see *Serious, overly*)

Still: Sandalwood, Arborvitae, Anti-Aging Blend, Reassuring Blend

Strengthened: Birch, Protective Blend, Wintergreen, Grounding Blend, Soothing Blend, Basil, Peppermint

Stressed: Massage Blend, Restful Blend, Ylang Ylang, Tension Blend, Basil, Vetiver, Red Mandarin, Holiday Blend, Sunshine Blend

Stubborn: Wintergreen, Oregano

Stuck: Cypress, Lemongrass, Thyme, Birch, Fennel, Cilantro, Ginger, Cleansing Blend, Detoxification Blend, Cellular Blend, Encouraging Blend, Sunshine Blend, Neroli

Suffering: Manuka, Uplifting Blend, Women's Blend

Superficial: Black Pepper, Oregano, Coriander, Kumquat

Supported: Birch, Cedarwood, Arborvitae, Roman Chamomile, Respiratory Blend, Manuka

Suppressing: Topical Blend, Copaiba, Geranium

Surrender: Wintergreen, Spikenard, Sandalwood, Arborvitae

Sympathetic: Neroli, Geranium, Marjoram, Renewing Blend

T

Teachable: Wintergreen, Oregano, Rosemary

Tenderhearted: Geranium, Ylang Ylang, Rose

Tense: Massage Blend, Tension Blend, Cypress, Lavender, Monthly Blend, Restful Blend

Terrified: Juniper Berry

Thankful: (see *Grateful*)

Timid: (see *Shy*)

Tired: (see *Exhausted*)

Tolerant: Thyme, Geranium, Soothing Blend, Cardamom, Renewing Blend, Neroli

Toxic: Lemongrass, Melaleuca, Cleansing Blend, Detoxification Blend, Cilantro, Lime, Thyme, Cellular Blend

Transforming: Helichrysum, Soothing Blend, Joyful Blend, Anti-Aging Blend, Cellular Blend

Transitioning: (see *Adjusting*)

Trapped: Petitgrain, Lavender, Thyme, Cleansing Blend, Cilantro, Black Pepper, Detoxification Blend, Eucalyptus, Jasmine, Joyful Blend

Traumatized: Hope Blend, Geranium, Clove, Helichrysum, Ylang Ylang, Jasmine, Comforting Blend

Trusting: Geranium, Marjoram, Myrrh, Rosemary, Jasmine, Cypress, Arborvitae, Respiratory Blend, Anti-Aging Blend, Rose, Manuka

U

Unashamed: Cassia, Copaiba

Unattractive: Grapefruit, Metabolic Blend

Unclean: Frankincense, Detoxification, Purification, Lemongrass

Unconscious: Petitgrain, Marjoram, Outdoor Blend

Understanding: Thyme, Cardamom, Renewing Blend

Unfocused: Lemon, Peppermint, Focus Blend

Unforgiving: Thyme, Geranium, Renewing Blend, Rose

Unfulfilled: Roman Chamomile, Jasmine, Neroli, Litsea

Ungrateful: Spikenard, Wild Orange, Helichrysum, Tension Blend, Douglas Fir, Lime

Ungrounded: Grounding Blend, Patchouli, Vetiver

Unheard: Lavender

Unkind: (see *Mean*)

Unloved: Bergamot, Respiratory Blend, Lavender, Rose, Jasmine, Hope Blend

Unloving: Geranium, Rose, Thyme

Unmotivated: Encouraging Blend, Invigorating Blend, Blue Tansy, Litsea, Black Pepper, Dill

Unnurtured: Myrrh

Unprotected: Protective Blend, Outdoor Blend, Frankincense, Manuka

Unsafe: Myrrh, Protective Blend, Jasmine, Frankincense, Melaleuca, Manuka, Reassuring Blend

Unseen: (see *Hiding*)

Unsettled: Roman Chamomile, Comforting Blend

Unsupported: Birch, Cedarwood, Arborvitae

Unsympathetic: Neroli, Geranium

Unteachable: Rosemary, Oregano

Unworthy: Copaiba, Cassia, Hope Blend, Metabolic Blend

Unyielding: (see *Stubborn*)

Upheld: Manuka

Uplifted: Uplifting Blend, Melissa, Tangerine

V

Valued: (see *Worthy*)

Victim mentality: Clove, Ginger, Spikenard, Jasmine, Protective Blend, Copaiba

Violated: Protective Blend, Ginger, Clove, Jasmine

Violent: Reassuring Blend, Frankincense, Cardamom

Vulnerable: Monthly Blend, Protective Blend, Outdoor Blend, Jasmine

W

Weak-willed: Petitgrain, Birch, Melaleuca, Ginger, Clove, Wintergreen

Weary: (see *Exhausted*)

Well: Eucalyptus, Patchouli, Fennel

Whole: Helichrysum, Manuka, Rose, Copaiba, Comforting Blend

Willful: Oregano, Wintergreen, Arborvitae

Wisdom: Douglas Fir, Frankincense, Petitgrain, Siberian Fir

Withdrawn: (see *Isolated*)

Workaholic: Wild Orange, Ylang Ylang, Tangerine, Basil, Tension Blend, White Fir

Worried: Wild Orange, Tangerine, Sandalwood, Cilantro, Massage Blend, Joyful Blend

Worthless: Cassia, Bergamot, Metabolic Blend

Worthy: Bergamot, Metabolic Blend, Topical Blend, Copaiba

Wounded: Helichrysum, Manuka, Jasmine, Soothing Blend